App Inventor 2 Essentials

A step-by-step introductory guide to mobile app
development with App Inventor 2

Felicia Kamriani

Krishnendu Roy

BIRMINGHAM - MUMBAI

App Inventor 2 Essentials

Copyright © 2016 Packt Publishing

First published: April 2016

Production reference: 1050416

Published by Packt Publishing Ltd.
Livery Place
35 Livery Street
Birmingham B3 2PB, UK.

ISBN 978-1-78528-110-5

www.packtpub.com

Credits

Authors

Felicia Kamriani

Krishnendu Roy

Reviewer

Sergio Martínez-Losa del Rincón

Commissioning Editor

Veena Pagare

Acquisition Editor

Reshma Raman

Content Development Editor

Anish Dhurat

Technical Editors

Chinmay Puranik

Parag Topre

Copy Editor

Akshata Lobo

Project Coordinator

Bijal Patel

Proofreader

Safis Editing

Indexer

Monica Ajmera Mehta

Graphics

Disha Haria

Production Coordinator

Conidon Miranda

Cover Work

Conidon Miranda

About the Authors

Felicia Kamriani is passionate about global education, empowering people with technology and closing the gender gap in STEM education. As Education and Business Development Manager, she evangelized the MIT App Inventor Project in the U.S. and abroad at the Google Rise Summit, the UNESCO YouthMobile conference, Guangzhou Educational Information Center, Hong Kong Polytech University, Guilin University, Samsung App Academy, MERLOT and MOSTEC. She also lead a team of Master Trainers for the Verizon Innovative App Challenge and spearheaded the inaugural MIT App Inventor Master Trainers Program for Mobile Computing Education. Other global endeavors include MOOC research and course development at HarvardX and with The Felittle Group, LLC, as Creative Director (www.felittlepeople.com). She is an avid TEDx organizer and proud alum of Harvard University, Stanford University and the University of California, Berkeley.

Krishnendu Roy is an associate professor of computer science at Valdosta State University. Prior to joining VSU, Krishnendu completed his PhD. and M.S. in computer engineering at Louisiana State University, Baton Rouge, LA in 2009 and 2005, respectively. As an MIT App Inventor Master Trainer, Krishnendu taught computing using App Inventor in summer camps for middle and high school students and in CS0 courses at his university. He has conducted in-person App Inventor workshops for teachers, including Google CS4HS and the University of Massachusetts at Boston's BATEC Summer Institute. He has also organized online App Inventor workshops for teachers who were involved in AAUW's Tech Trek camps and mentored national winning teams of Verizon's Innovative App Challenge.

About the Reviewer

Sergio Martínez-Losa del Rincón lives in Spain. He is a software engineer and an entrepreneur.

He always likes to write technical documents as well as programming in several languages. He is always learning new programming languages and facing new challenges. Currently, he is creating applications and games for iPhone, Macintosh, Android, GoogleGlass, Unity3D, and Cocos2D-X. He likes VR technologies and all kinds of challenges. He also likes web programming and designing good APIs for mobile applications.

So far, he has developed all kinds of applications in Java, C++, Objective-C, PHP, and other languages. He is now developing products inside the IoT field using SaaS technologies. He likes to explore cloud services to expand application possibilities. He also likes machine learning technologies and natural language processing to study new ways to use big data.

You can see part of his work here: `http://goo.gl/k5tOSX`.

www.PacktPub.com

eBooks, discount offers, and more

Did you know that Packt offers eBook versions of every book published, with PDF and ePub files available? You can upgrade to the eBook version at www.PacktPub.com and as a print book customer, you are entitled to a discount on the eBook copy. Get in touch with us at customercare@packtpub.com for more details.

At www.PacktPub.com, you can also read a collection of free technical articles, sign up for a range of free newsletters and receive exclusive discounts and offers on Packt books and eBooks.

https://www2.packtpub.com/books/subscription/packtlib

Do you need instant solutions to your IT questions? PacktLib is Packt's online digital book library. Here, you can search, access, and read Packt's entire library of books.

Why subscribe?

- Fully searchable across every book published by Packt
- Copy and paste, print, and bookmark content
- On demand and accessible via a web browser

Table of Contents

Preface   **v**

Chapter 1: Unleashing Creativity with MIT App Inventor 2   **1**

What is MIT App Inventor 2?   **2**

Understanding your role as a mobile app developer   3

Brainstorming app ideas   4

The Design Thinking process   4

Empathize   5

Define   6

Ideate   6

Prototype   7

Test   7

Computational thinking   8

Best practices to design apps   8

MIT App Inventor – purpose and potential   **9**

Discovering the possibilities of MIT App Inventor   10

MIT App Inventor examples   11

Stopwatch and Timer   11

Yahtzee   12

BYJ3S   12

Loops   13

Quartet   14

Brain Reaction Accelerator   14

ConstHelp – Contractor Tools   15

UMATI   16

Ez School Bus Locator   17

Youth Radio   17

Rover 800 Remote   18

Summary   **19**

Chapter 2: Setting Up MIT App Inventor 2   21

The initial setup   22
System requirements   22
Signing up a Google account   23
Logging in to MIT App Inventor   23

Connectivity setup   27
Downloading the AI2 Companion app   27
Connecting your computer and Android device with WiFi   29
Connecting the emulator or connecting using a USB cable   31
Step 1 – installing the App Inventor setup software   31
Step 2 – launch aiStarter   41
Step 3 – opening a project and connecting to the emulator   41
Step 4 – setting up your device with a USB cable   43
Step 5 – connecting your computer and device (authenticating if necessary)   44
Step 6 – testing the connection   45

Summary   45

Chapter 3: Navigating the App Inventor Platform   47

The projects view   48
Creating a new project   48

The Designer   49
Palette   50
Viewer   50
Components   50
Properties   51
Media   51

Creating a game app   51
Creating the UI in designer   52
IDE   60

The Blocks editor   71
The Blocks drawer   72
Types of Blocks   73
Using Blocks to program Fling   73

Summary   92

Chapter 4: Fling App – Part 2   93

Adding a scoring feature   95
Coding scoring blocks   95
Updating the score label   98

Increasing difficulty   100

Changing the game's dynamic   101

Creating levels   103

Updating the score label to display the level	**108**
Updating the Reset button	**111**
Updating the Play button	**115**
Summary	**117**
Chapter 5: Building an Event App	**119**
User Interface for an event app	**120**
Setting the background image	**120**
Adding an image component	**124**
Adding buttons	**126**
Adding the ActivityStarter	**130**
Adding screens	**133**
Programming the blocks	**134**
Navigating between screens and launching maps	134
Screen1	134
Sharing blocks between screens using the Backpack	135
Adding text to screens	138
Summary	**139**
Chapter 6: Introduction to Databases	**141**
Creating a database	**142**
Creating a Google Fusion Table	142
Designing the RSVP screen	**149**
Creating the GUI in the designer window	149
Setting up Google Authentication	**153**
Sharing the Fusion Table with the service account email	**159**
Connecting the app to the Google Fusion Table	**161**
Our goal	161
Pushing data to the Fusion Table	**163**
Ensuring empty rows are not inserted	**166**
Viewing the guest list	**168**
Coding the blocks – requesting data	**169**
Coding the blocks – receiving data	**169**
Sharing the Event App	**171**
Summary	**172**
Chapter 7: Learning About Loops with a Raffle App	**173**
Creating the project and building the GUI	**174**
Creating a new project	174
Creating the User Interface (UI)	175
Programming the behavior of the Digital Raffle app	179
Creating and initializing the variable and list	180

Receiving text messages from participants	182
Adding the phone numbers of all the participants to the list	185
Selecting a winner	187
Notifying the winner	189
Notifying everyone else	190
Using loops	193
Clearing out the list and variable	196
Summary	**197**
Chapter 8: Expanding Your Mobile App Development Skills	**199**
Design principles	**199**
User-centered design	200
Visual hierarchy	200
Responsive design	201
Research app markets	202
Design tools	203
App Inventor extras	**203**
Shortcuts	204
Help	204
Titles	206
Images	207
Virtual screens	207
Backups	214
Distributing your app	**215**
The App Inventor Gallery	215
Viewing the Gallery apps	215
Sharing your app in the Gallery	216
Creating an AIA file	217
Downloading and sharing	218
Creating an APK	218
QR code	219
Direct download (or side-loading)	220
The Google Play Store	220
Summary	**222**
Index	**225**

Preface

Almost everyone has had an idea for an app or perhaps declared, "I wish there were an app for that!" But until recently, taking an idea and building it into a fully functional app would have required hiring an expert software programmer and paying thousands and thousands of dollars. The world of mobile app development had been the domain of an elite group of people with highly specialized skills — proficient coders. The App Inventor project sought to change this reality by democratizing software development. App Inventor 2 is a free, blocks-based, drag-and-drop visual programming language that makes it possible for anyone, even people with no prior coding experience, to turn an idea into a fully functional Android app.

As educators, our passion for promoting global education and empowering people to move from being users of technology to becoming creators of technology were the inspirations for writing this book. With App Inventor, a 12-year-old, a speech therapist, a baseball coach, or anyone else for that matter, can develop an app that is personal, meaningful, and useful to them. People from all backgrounds and levels of education can develop a digital solution to a problem they see in their community. Any App Inventor app, such as an educational game, a music tutorial, or a garbage recycling program can be published or sold in app markets, and thus, have a global impact or spurn opportunities for entrepreneurship, collaboration, and community building.

App Inventor offers an alternative entry point to Computer Science that is more user-friendly and less intimidating than traditional cryptic white-text-on-a-black-screen programming. The colorful blocks that snap together like puzzle pieces along with a design tools enable users to learn both coding and user experience design skills. Furthermore, with a wide gender gap in computer science — males dominating both classes and jobs — we are also passionate about using App Inventor to introduce more girls and women to mobile computing opportunities, such as app contests with Technovation (www.technovationchallenge.org) and coding clubs with Girls Who Code (www.girlswhocode.com).

Because you can take any idea and turn it into a mobile app, the opportunities for imagination, creativity, and innovation are indeed endless. The purpose of this book is to help spark such creativity while introducing you to basic computer science principles, computational thinking, and programming. This book teaches you to navigate the App Inventor platform and helps you become familiar with its features through step-by-step tutorials on building three different mobile apps. Throughout the book, we offer design tools and tips as a pathway to user experience design, since the user interface is such an integral part of any mobile app. Ultimately, by the end of this book, you will be equipped with enough skills to embark on developing your own mobile app from scratch. We are excited to see the apps you are inspired to create and hope that you will share them with us.

We are so excited to share our passion for mobile app development with you and hope that this book awakens a creative spark to make technology that is personal, meaningful, and useful to you. We are thankful to Hal Abelson, Mark Friedman, and all of the original App Inventor developers and visionaries who created the platform that has evolved into App Inventor 2. We are proud to be furthering the App Inventor mission and encourage all of you budding software programmers to, in turn, share App Inventor with other noncoders. Together we can empower others to become part of a growing movement to connect and impact the world with digital creativity.

> *"We look forward to hearing about the digital solutions you devise or your evolution in the mobile computing space. Good luck and keep connecting!"*

> *– Felicia Kamriani and Krishsnendu Roy*

What this book covers

Chapter 1, Unleashing Creativity with MIT App Inventor 2, introduces you to the MIT App Inventor software and explores the multifaceted role of the mobile app developer by examining design processes and techniques used to turn an app idea into a prototype. By showing a variety of apps that people just like you have already made, this chapter reveals the range of learning outcomes and skills developed by using App Inventor.

Chapter 2, Setting Up MIT App Inventor 2, walks you through setting up a Google Account to log into App Inventor, downloading software, and connecting your computer to your mobile device via Wi-Fi or USB with Mac, Windows, or GNU/ Linux. MIT App Inventor 2 is a free online application that runs in a web browser on your computer and saves your projects in the cloud. The magical part of App Inventor is live testing your app as you build it with the **Integrated Development Environment (IDE)**. If you don't have a mobile device, don't worry, there are instructions on how to use App Inventor with the onscreen emulator. While we provide a step-by-step guide to getting started, we acknowledge that sometimes establishing connectivity can be a challenge. Therefore, we include plenty of troubleshooting and help options.

Chapter 3, Navigating the App Inventor Platform, familiarizes you with the App Inventor Projects View, Designer screen, and Blocks Editor. This chapter teaches you how to build a game app called Fling. The step-by-step tutorial integrates components and properties to design the user interface and colorful puzzle-like blocks to code the behavior of the game. You learn how to create buttons that start or reset play, move a ball, change the ball's direction by touching it, bounce the ball off the edges of the screen, and end game play. During each step of the development process, we show you how to view the changes on your mobile device. By the end of the chapter, you will have built a functional app! However, we have just gotten started on our app development journey.

Chapter 4, Fling App – Part 2, uses the basic app that we built in *Chapter 3* as a launching pad for further skill development: debugging and expanding the app with more complex features. Since most games keep score and have increasing levels and difficulty, we augment the Fling tutorial to make a more intermediate app. You learn how to make a scoring mechanism, display the score, increase the speed of the ball, create levels, increase the difficulty of play, and debug by updating the Play and Reset buttons.

Chapter 5, Building an Event App, provides a tutorial for building a second app— this time, an intermediate event-planning app. An app like this can be useful for anyone who is gathering people together for meetings, parties, or events. It gathers information from people who would like to attend, namely, their name, the number of guests, and the pot-luck items to be brought. In return, the app displays to users a guest list and the event information, such as the address and a map. The tutorial teaches you how to include images and artwork, create a navigation menu, use the Backpack tool, add multiple screens, expand your use of labels, and include a map component. By the end of the chapter, you will have accomplished a great deal, but will only be halfway through the Event App development.

Chapter 6, Introduction to Databases, will cover databases that are an essential part of app designing because they store persistent data, meaning that when the app closes and reopens, the previously entered data will remain in the App. Without a database, any data entered by the user when the app is running would be lost once the app is closed. In order to collect user-inputted information for the Event app, this chapter's tutorial demonstrates how to create an RSVP form, establish Google API credentials, store and request information in a database using Google Fusion Tables, and display a guest list.

Chapter 7, Learning About Loops with a Raffle App, will cover a third tutorial—this time, for a Raffle App that includes the computer science principles of lists, loops, and variables. The Raffle App (a digital version of a regular raffle) can be used at a party, meeting break, or as an ice-breaker to involve participants in a short fun activity. Participants text a specific message to the Raffle organizer's phone and the app randomly selects a winner from the list of incoming numbers and then notifies the winner he or she has won and texts the rest of the participants that they did not win. Here, you will learn to code efficiently with variables and a loop, as the app repeats the same behavior (texting a "Sorry you did not win!" message) for a list of many people.

Chapter 8, Expanding Your Mobile App Development Skills, includes more design principles and App Inventor tips to broaden your skill set for your transition from app building with guided tutorials to creating mobile apps from scratch. Also included are app sharing tools that enable you to contribute your creativity and learn from other app developers. Since all the App Inventor apps can be uploaded, shared, and even sold in app markets, the apps you develop can make a global social impact or trigger your path as an entrepreneur. The world awaits your contribution!

What you need to build mobile apps

- A free Google Account
- An Android mobile device (phone or tablet)
    - Android Operating System 2.3 ("Gingerbread") or higher
- A computer with one of the operating systems listed:
    - Macintosh (with Intel processor): Mac OS X 10.5 or higher
    - Windows: Windows XP, Windows Vista, Windows 7, 8, or 10
    - GNU/Linux: Ubuntu 8 or higher, Debian 5 or higher

- A web browser:
  - Mozilla Firefox 3.6 or higher (Note: If you are using Firefox with the **NoScript** extension, you'll need to turn the extension off. See the note on the troubleshooting page.)
  - Apple Safari 5.0 or higher
  - Google Chrome 4.0 or higher
  - Microsoft Internet Explorer is not supported. Windows users should use Chrome or Firefox

Who this book is for

This book is for anyone wanting to learn how to create mobile apps for Android. No prior coding experience is necessary.

Conventions

In this book, you will find a number of text styles that distinguish between different kinds of information. Here are some examples of these styles and an explanation of their meaning.

Code words in text, database table names, folder names, filenames, file extensions, pathnames, dummy URLs, user input, and Twitter handles are shown as follows: "The file is named `appinventor2-setup_1.1.tar.gz` and it is a GZIP compressed TAR file."

Any command-line input or output is written as follows:

```
> /usr/google/appinventor/commands-for-Appinventor/aiStarter &
```

New terms and **important words** are shown in bold. Words that you see on the screen, for example, in menus or dialog boxes, appear in the text like this: "There are five games to choose from, including **Refocus**, **True Color**, **Quick Pick**, **Sum It Up**, and **Expression Puzzle**."

 Warnings or important notes appear in a box like this.

 Tips and tricks appear like this.

Reader feedback

Feedback from our readers is always welcome. Let us know what you think about this book—what you liked or found challenging. Reader feedback is important to us as it helps us develop resources that you will find useful and educational.

To send us general feedback, simply e-mail feedback@packtpub.com, and mention the book's title in the subject of your message.

If there is a topic that you have expertise in and you are interested in either writing or contributing to a book, see our author guide at www.packtpub.com/authors.

Customer support

Now that you are the proud owner of a Packt book, we have a number of things to help you to get the most from your purchase.

Errata

Although we have taken every care to ensure the accuracy of our content, mistakes do happen. If you find a mistake in one of our books—maybe a mistake in the text or the code—we would be grateful if you could report this to us. By doing so, you can save other readers from frustration and help us improve subsequent versions of this book. If you find any errata, please report them by visiting http://www.packtpub.com/submit-errata, selecting your book, clicking on the **Errata Submission Form** link, and entering the details of your errata. Once your errata are verified, your submission will be accepted and the errata will be uploaded to our website or added to any list of existing errata under the Errata section of that title.

To view the previously submitted errata, go to https://www.packtpub.com/books/content/support and enter the name of the book in the search field. The required information will appear under the **Errata** section.

Piracy

Piracy of copyrighted material on the Internet is an ongoing problem across all media. At Packt, we take the protection of our copyright and licenses very seriously. If you come across any illegal copies of our works in any form on the Internet, please provide us with the location address or website name immediately so that we can pursue a remedy.

Please contact us at `copyright@packtpub.com` with a link to the suspected pirated material.

We appreciate your help in protecting our authors and our ability to bring you valuable content.

Questions

If you have an issue with any aspect of this book, you can contact us at `questions@packtpub.com`, and we will do our best to address the problem.

1
Unleashing Creativity with MIT App Inventor 2

Mobile applications are ubiquitous. There are apps for just about everything—entertainment, socializing, dining, travel, philanthropy, shopping, education, navigation, and so on. And just about everyone with a smartphone or tablet is using them to make their lives easier or better. But you have decided to move from just using mobile apps to creating mobile apps. Congratulations! Thanks to MIT App Inventor 2, mobile app development is no longer exclusively the realm of experienced software programmers. The software empowers anyone with an idea to create mobile technology. This book offers people of all ages a step-by-step guide to creating mobile apps with MIT App Inventor 2. While this visual programming language is an ideal tool for people who have little or no coding experience, don't be fooled into thinking that the software's capabilities are basic! The simple drag-and-drop blocks format is actually a powerful programming language capable of creating complex and sophisticated mobile apps.

The purpose of this chapter is to provide an overview of MIT App Inventor 2, and of your new role as a mobile app developer. You are in for more skill development than you ever imagined! Of course, you will learn to code mobile apps, but there are countless other valuable skills weaved into the mobile app building process. Most significantly, you will learn to think differently, discover the design-thinking process, become a problem solver, and be resourceful. This chapter also offers tips on design principles and brainstorming app ideas. Lastly, it reveals the potential of MIT App Inventor 2 and showcases an array of mobile apps so that you, a budding app designer, can begin thinking about the full spectrum of possibilities. These mobile app examples not only display the capabilities and functionalities of MIT App Inventor 2, but also serve to spark ideas, foster innovative thinking, and help create visual goals as you embark on the mobile app-making process in the next chapters.

This chapter covers the following topics:

- What is MIT App Inventor 2 and why you should learn to use it?
- Becoming a mobile app developer
- Discovering the possibilities of MIT App Inventor 2

What is MIT App Inventor 2?

MIT App Inventor 2 is a free, drag-and-drop, blocks-based visual programming language that enables people, regardless of their coding experience, to create mobile apps for Android devices. In 2008, iPhones and Android phones had just hit the market. MIT professor Hal Abelson had the idea to create an easy-to-use programming language to make mobile apps that would harness the power of the emerging smartphone technology. Equipped with fast processors, large memory storage, and sensors, smartphones were enabling people to monitor and interact with their environment like never before. Abelson's goal was to democratize the mobile app development process by making it easy for anyone to create mobile apps that were meaningful and important to them. While on sabbatical at Google in Mountain View, CA, Abelson worked with Engineer Mark Friedman and many of other developers to create App Inventor (yes, it was originally called Google App Inventor).

In 2011, Abelson brought App Inventor to MIT and, together with the Media Lab and the **CSAIL** (Computer Science and Artificial Intelligence Lab), created the Center for Mobile Learning. In December 2013, Abelson and his team of developers launched MIT App Inventor 2 (from here on referred to as MIT App Inventor), an even easier to use web-based application version featuring an Integrated Development Environment (IDE). IDE means that you as you build your mobile app online, you can see it come to life on a connected mobile device. All you need is a computer (Mac or PC), an Internet connection (or a USB connection), a Google account, and an Android device (phone or tablet). But, if you don't have an Android device, don't worry! You can still create apps with the onscreen emulator and utilize the live development mode.

The MIT App Inventor (http://appinventor.mit.edu/) interface includes two main screens, a Designer Screen, which is a graphical user interface (GUI) where you can create the look and feel of the app (choosing the components you want the app to include), and the Blocks Editor, where you can add behavior to the app by coding it with colorful blocks. Users build apps by dragging components and blocks from the menu bars onto a workspaces (called Viewers) and a connected Android device (or emulator) displays the progress in real time. All the apps are saved on the MIT server; once completed, they can be can be shared on the MIT App Inventor Gallery, submitted to app contests (such as MIT App of the Month), or uploaded to the Google Play Store (or other app marketplaces) for sharing or selling.

To date, MIT App Inventor has empowered millions of people to become creators of technology by learning to be mobile app developers. And now, you will become one of them!

Understanding your role as a mobile app developer

Since you are reading this book, it is safe to assume that not only do you regularly use mobile apps, but on occasion, you have also had the thought, "I wish there were an app for that!" Now, with the help of MIT App Inventor and this guidebook to mobile app development, you will soon be able to say, "I can create an app for that!"

While embracing your new role as a mobile app developer, you will not just be learning how to code; you will learn an array of other valuable skills. You will learn to think differently. Every time you open an app, you will start looking at it from the developer's perspective rather than just as a user. You will start noticing what functions are logical and simple and which are complicated and unintuitive. You will learn to get inspiration from your environment. What type of app could make the attendance process at my club/class/meeting more streamlined or efficient? What app idea could help solve the inaccurate inventory problem at the gym? You will learn to become a data gatherer without even realizing it. When people make comments about apps, your ears will perk up and you will take note. You will start asking questions like, why do you prefer Waze over Google Maps?

You will learn to become a problem solver. You will learn to think logically so that you can tell the computer in a step-by-step manner how to perform an operation. Any software developer will confirm that programming is an iterative process. It's a continual cycle of coding, troubleshooting, and debugging. Trial and error will become second nature, as will taking a step back to figure out why something that just worked a minute ago now seems broken. And, you will learn to assume the role of a designer. It is no longer accurate to merely depict programmers holed up by themselves at a computer, creating white text-based code on black screens. Developers of mobile apps are also designers who think about and create attractive and intuitive user interfaces (UIs). Much of the design work happens not at the computer; it includes conversations with potential users, involves pens, paper, and post-it notes, and uses storyboards or sketches. Only once you have your app designed on paper do you sit down at the computer to begin coding. And then, you will not find the traditional black and white interface, as the MIT App Inventor platform is interactive and full of colorful blocks that snap together.

Brainstorming app ideas

Chances are you already have an idea for a mobile app. If not, how can you think of one? The best way to start brainstorming app ideas is by starting with what you know. Which app do you wish existed? Which app would you and your friends, coworkers, or family members use, need, or like? Which problem in your community, network, or circle of friends could be solved with a digital solution? Maybe, you loan out books to friends, but don't have a system to keep track of who borrowed what. Maybe, you want to do a clothing swap with people who are your size, so you want to post pictures of the items that you have available for trade and you want to view othe listed items in your size. Maybe, you have a favorite app that you use all the time, but you wish it had just one other feature. Maybe, when you meet your friends in a public place, it's hard to know whether they're nearby without a lot of texting back and forth, so you want to create an app that shows everyone's location on one screen. The possibilities are endless!

The key to successful brainstorming is to write down all of your ideas no matter how wild they are and then talk to people about them to get feedback. Input from others is an essential part of the research needed to ensure that your app idea becomes a successful app that people will want, use, and/or buy. On a recent business trip, we had an idea for a travel app because we always seem to forget at least one essential item. Over breakfast at the hotel, we discussed the app idea with a couple of colleagues and received amazing insights that we hadn't thought of, such as a reminder notification to fill any prescriptions well before the trip and a weather component, so we could be sure to pack appropriate clothes for each destination. The more people you talk to, the more market research you will conduct and the more defined the overall app's concept will be.

The Design Thinking process

Design Thinking (more information about Design Thinking can be found at `http://dschool.stanford.edu`) is a user-centered process for creative problem solving. While not developed specifically for mobile app development, the Design Thinking process is particularly effective when applied to mobile app development. We recommend using the following design phases:

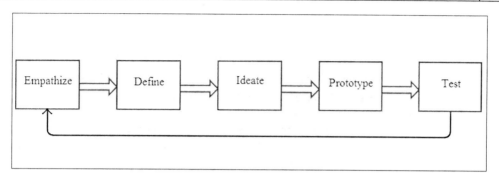

Most likely, you are not creating an app that you alone will use, so you must discover what potential users need, want, or prefer in an app.

Empathize

Your first goal is to understand the people who would be using your app. Thus, this phase is called, Empathize. You can easily conduct research through interviews by asking an array of potential users what types of apps they currently use, what app features they like or dislike, what apps they wish existed, and if they would use an app like the one you plan on making. Interviews can provide valuable feedback and be a source of inspiration for new ideas.

For example, if you plan to create a book club app that coordinates many people's calendars so that you can schedule a book club discussion during a time when everyone is available, ask book club members what features they would like to see in the app. Will there be an RSVP or a cancel button? Will there be directions to the location? What are the transportation or parking options? Will there be a link to Amazon to buy or download the next month's book? How can the app help members decide on which book to read next? Since the meetings are potlucks, is there an option to include what food or drink each member will bring? What is a quick and efficient way to contact all the members? Through this data gathering stage, you may discover a wealth of new features for your app that you had not previously thought of, or you may get a confirmation that you are indeed on the right track. Understanding what potential users want is an essential part of the app building process, from the very beginning of concept creation all the way until the final stage of deployment.

Define

Once you've gathered research data, what do you do with that information and how do you fold it into your design? In the **Define** phase, you will synthesize the data you've collected to create a clearer picture of what your app will do, how it will function, and the purpose it will serve. You may have collected pages and pages of ideas and comments from your interviews. What themes or patterns emerge when reviewing them? What ideas seem the most salient? What app functions were people most excited about? Reviewing user feedback will help you structure and streamline your app concept so that it is clear and specific in purpose and function. This stage of flushing out ideas so the best ones emerge will also help you create accurate visuals in the next phase.

Ideate

Given all of the input you need and want from your potential users, what solutions can your app offer? Now, it is time for the **Ideate** phase to create an experience map or storyboard with pen, paper, and post-its to delineate all of the app's functionalities. Each piece of paper will represent one screen and display the user interface (UI) designated for that screen. This process usually requires a lot of revisions and may produce numerous versions of the app, which you will want to keep, as they may be helpful down the line when creating updates. We find it helpful to put all of the drawings up on a wall so that you can visualize the whole app map and its sequencing. This is also the time to include design features that you like or find appealing. Remember, all of the apps you see in marketplaces started the exact same way, with an idea. Inspiration for one can come at any time and from any experience. We recommend dedicating a notebook exclusively for ideas, so you can jot notes when you get inspired or see an app with a look and feel that you like. This will be a valuable resource for you as you continue down the road of app making. As with any design process, this **Ideate** stage takes time. This is a good thing because you want time for your ideas to simmer and percolate. Taking a break and coming back to your sketches with fresh eyes usually offers new perspectives , ideas and clarity.

Prototype

Now that you've reached the **Prototype** phase, it is time to sit down at the computer and build your app. This may be daunting at first because you are just learning how to use MIT App Inventor, but the step-by-step guides in this book will walk you through each stage of app development. The provided tutorials will teach you about the various MIT App Inventor components, what they do, and how to add behavior to them by snapping blocks together. Once you become familiar with component functions and get the hang of coding with blocks, you will be able to transfer this knowledge to create your own app. Since you will have already done all of the phases of the the Design Thinking process in this chapter and laid the groundwork for your app, you will be able to particularly concentrate on the components you will need to build your app.

Test

When you get to the point where you think your app is done, think again! **Test** your app with a small group of users before offering it to the world in an app marketplace. These alpha and beta testers will help you discover bugs or if things are not working as they should. Learning to troubleshoot is often a frustrating process; but by this stage, you will have refined your skills as a problem solver, and you will have more ideas on how to fix bugs. Also, *Chapter 8, Expanding Your Mobile App Development Skills*, of is devoted to tools to expand your app development skills. And while the **Test** phase seems like the final one, you will discover that it is really another beginning! The Design Thinking process is really a cyclical one, as there is always room for edits, refinement, and of course, version 2.

If you get stuck at any time, there are many resources on the MIT App Inventor websites at, `http://appinventor.mit.edu/` and on `http://www.appinventor.org/` to help you. In addition to tutorials, there is an MIT App Inventor Gallery where you can view apps along with the source codes that other people have created and shared. If an app has features that you'd like to include in your app but you don't know how to code yet, you can download the app, look at the blocks, and teach yourself how to code them! Also, there is a community forum online where you can ask questions and learn from more experienced users.

Computational thinking

In becoming a mobile app developer, you will be learning many valuable roles: brainstormer observer, researcher, data interpreter, synthesizer, design architect, strategist, creative thinker, and last, but not least, coder. Part of becoming a mobile app developer involves learning to think like a computer, that is, being able to tell the computer what you want it to do so that it performs the specific operation. Computers are not intuitive; they don't know what you mean or interpret what you say. By programming or writing a code, you give the computer clear step-by-step logical instructions to make it do something that you want it to do, such as retrieve data, display information, or open another application. But sometimes, even when you think you are being clear and logical, the computer does not respond as you intended. As coding is an iterative process, there are a lot of rounds of trying something to see if it works, and then when it doesn't, trying something else. The more you fail, the closer you will get to finding a successful path. Learning to troubleshoot, debug a program, or think of yet another *solution* comes with the willingness to be open, think creatively, and try and try again. You will soon discover that by becoming a coder, you are also honing your skills as a problem solver.

Best practices to design apps

Since there is an abundance of Android apps that are available, you can easily research design principles.

Pay attention to all the features of the UIs. For example, look at 10 different chess game, solitaire, or weather apps. You will see a wide variety of UIs and start learning how different developers approach the exact same app. Which ones are easy to navigate and use? What distinguishes one as more appealing than another? Which home screens provide the best overview of an app's set of features? How are menus and drawers displayed? How easy is it to return to the previous screen? How do you navigate to the home screen? How are text elements highlighted when in use? How are screens mapped out? Where can you find instructions? Where do you find help? Pay attention to cues, such as what colors, animations, or pop-up messaging occur, to let you know that X is happening.

Great design is simple. Often, the tendency is to want your app to do it all. You've received tons of feedback from your interviews and you want to incorporate all of the brilliant ideas into your app. Since this is your first app-making experience with MIT App Inventor, we recommend you to choose the core features that are necessary, and make them clear and easy to use. If needed, you can always layer more complex features in the future versions. Think about your own app usage. Most of us use apps very quickly or intermittently (unless we are on a long subway ride, playing a game on our phone or reading a digital book). Rarely do you use all of the features of an app at any given time. Most often, you use an app for a specific purpose and then you're done. Keep your app simple.

Iterate, iterate, and iterate. Designing, like coding, requires the ability to be open to experimentation. And fortunately, App Inventor facilitates this process with instant feedback through IDE. Try a component, add behavior (blocks), and see what happens on your connected device. Add a different behavior; see what happens on your connected device. Add colors, arrangements, and fonts; see what happens on your connected device. Do you get the drill? Design involves a lot of trials, errors, and failures, which is ultimately a good thing because it gets you going in a different direction. You may have your heart set on a design idea only to discover that, once you have tried it out, you don't like it that much. Don't be discouraged! This is the time to investigate other options. Try this, that, and the other. Expand your creative scope through several rounds of playing and then testing.

App designing, like any artistic endeavor, takes time. Try not to rush the creative process. Indeed, MIT App Inventor makes it easy to make mobile apps, but to craft a well-designed app that looks appealing and works seamlessly requires the investment of time, passion, and creativity. Take breaks often, spend time outdoors, play a game or engage your mind in another project so that when you return to your app, you will approach it with fresh eyes, energy, thoughts, and inspiration.

MIT App Inventor – purpose and potential

While making apps with MIT App Inventor, there is much more going on than just learning to code. The mission of MIT App Inventor is to democratize coding so that everyone, regardless of age, schooling, or profession, has the opportunity to create technology. Coaches, players, teachers, students, doctors, patients, conductors, cellists, pilots, or passengers can all make mobile apps that are important to them and that make their lives happier, better, or more productive.

As a digital solution, your app may have originally been intended to solve a problem that you observed or experienced. But once you share it in an app marketplace, it could impact people you don't even know and may never meet. MIT App Inventor makes it possible for you to expand your scope of influence from your immediate local community to a worldwide scale. You can bring others joy and laughter with a simple game, you can help college-bound seniors study for a standardized test, or you can provide a tool that teaches travelers common phrases in other languages. Contributing positively to society is one awesome way to use your new rockstar MIT App Inventor skills.

As you begin creating apps and see the impact they have on others, you may broaden the scope of what you think is possible for yourself. Have you thought about becoming a social entrepreneur? Will people pay for the technology you have created? Does your app have the growth potential to serve new and different users? How can you expand your business acumen to learn how to build and market successful mobile apps? Even though you will be starting off with small and simple apps, always remember to dream big in what you do and who you are.

While MIT App Inventor offers an easy and approachable way to learn about coding and software development, it may indeed also serve as an on-ramp for further computer science education. Once you see the skill growth potential, such as how creating technology can positively impact others or that you can sell your digital solutions, you may indeed become interested in expanding your knowledge of technology further by delving into other software languages or science learning opportunities, such as maker-spaces or hackathons.

Discovering the possibilities of MIT App Inventor

MIT App Inventor empowers anyone regardless of age or coding experience to transform an app idea into a prototype and ultimately into a full-fledged mobile application. What will your app do? As you begin your app-making journey, you may wonder about what types of apps could you possibly create with App Inventor? Since the apps you make will be shared or sold for use on an Android smartphone or tablet, you can create apps that access the full functionality of those devices. Your apps could do things such as speak, take photos (or selfies), make phone calls, text, translate SMS messages, Tweet, play music or videos, use GPS (maps or other websites), scan bar codes, set timers (alarms or reminders), control robots, launch others apps, track your movement, and so on. Given the array of the abilities of Android devices, the possibilities seem endless!

MIT App Inventor examples

Before beginning to learn MIT App Inventor, we think it is helpful to review some examples MIT App Inventor apps so that you have an idea ahead of time of a range of possibilities. As you start learning MIT App Inventor, you can begin by making simple apps; but in the back of your mind, remember this array of app examples, as they can serve goals or be an inspiration to help you unlock your creativity and designing skills. Think of it this way if you want to become a watercolor painter, but have never painted before, you would look at many watercolor paintings made by professionals or people with more experience than you to get inspired, to have a visual of what is possible, and to learn how the paintings were created.

The following examples are a mix of beginning, intermediate, and advanced MIT App Inventor apps. Some were created by individuals, who were inspired to make a specific app, while others were created by groups of people for a project or as a contest submission. One thing all of these apps have in common is that before the app developers spent hours and hours perfecting their UIs and creating blocks of code, they were just like you, starting out with little or no previous coding experience. All of the skills you develop in this book through basic and intermediate app-making will serve as a solid foundation for you to build upon to be able to create more complex, sophisticated apps in the future. The introductory tutorials will teach you the MIT App Inventor basics and equip you to tackle app creation from scratch.

Stopwatch and Timer

Jari Pohjasmäki from Finland developed the following useful and simple *Stopwatch and Timer* app:

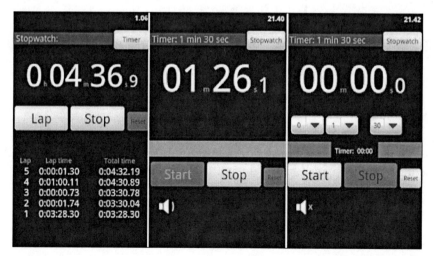

Components used: Button, Label, TextBox, Image, ListPicker, Arrangements, Clock, and Notifier

Yahtzee

This app mimics the classic game of *Yahtzee*, where the object of the game is to score points by rolling five dice. The dice can be rolled up to three times in a turn and the game will consist of 13 rounds. Each player scores their roll in one of the 13 categories. Once a category has been used, it cannot be used again. Rolling a *Yahtzee* is five-of-a-kind and scores 50 points; the highest of any category. Whoever scores most points will win!

The following screenshots show the total gameplay points for different roles of the dice:

Components used: Button, Label, Notifier, and Alignments

BYJ3S

Vicenta Albeldo and Jesus Gil created *BYJS3*, a digital pet game. This app allows you to play with, feed, and bathe your very own virtual pet. The following screenshots show the incorporated hand-drawn images that the developers have animated:

Components used: Clock, TinyDB, Image, Alignments, Canvas, and Sound

Loops

Developed by Andrea Zaffardi from Italy, *Loops* won the MIT App of the Month contest in June 2015. It is a puzzle game that requires the player to rotate the pipes to form a closed loop before time runs out. There are 100 levels of gameplay. The following screenshots show the game in the various stages:

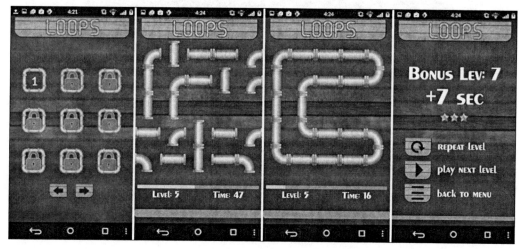

Components used: Image, Player, Clock, Sounds, TinyDB, Button, Label, Slider, and Alignments

Quartet

Dr. Arun Mehta from India created *Quartet* for his niece, who loves to dance, but hates math. He wanted to show her how math can convert movement into things, such as graphics and music. With a wave of the phone, the app plays music with as many as four instruments (piano, pan flute, strings, and tin drums) while displaying animated graphics. Music starts and stops with a simple screen touch. A button displays a list of instruments for the user to choose among. If just one instrument is selected, the app will play all of individual keys of that instrument. Moving the phone in different patterns will create new music!

The following screenshots show visuals as the app plays music:

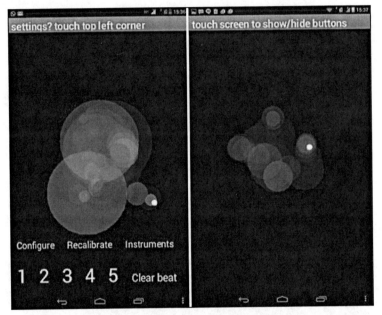

Components used: Accelerometer, Canvas, Ball, ImageSprite, Button, Label, Sound, Player, Alignments, and Animation

Brain Reaction Accelerator

Created by Meghraj Singh of India, *Brain Reaction Accelerator* is a puzzle app that provides brain teasers to be solved within a time frame. There are five games to choose from, including **Refocus**, **True Color**, **Quick Pick**, **Sum It Up**, and **Expression Puzzle**. Compete against your best score or among global users. The following screenshots show a sequence from registering to choosing and playing a game:

Components used: Button, Label, Alignments, ListPicker, TextField, Canvas, ImageSprite

ConstHelp – Contractor Tools

Created by Derek Drew from the United States, *Construction Calculator* is a tool for people on building sites. It performs unit conversions, assists with project management, provides a to-do list keeper, and measures distances. It has an autodialing feature for calling customers or vendors, but includes autotexting for safety while driving to or from a site. The following screenshots show the home screen, a screen to calculate volume, and a location screen:

Components used: Button, Label, WebViewer, LocationSensor, Alignments,
SMS Messaging, ListPicker, and TextField

UMATI

In the spring of 2015, MIT students Carolina Morgan, Fei Xu, Marcel Williams, and Rida Qadri created the mobile app *UMATI* for the urban planning course *11.S938: Crowd Sourced City – Social Media, Technology, and Planning Processes*. The class enabled students to work with actual planning and advocacy organizations to develop digital technology solutions for planning problems. Matatus bus routes in Nairobi were not standardized. They were often created and changed by the whim of private drivers or as a result of traffic conditions and it was difficult to know which buses traveled which routes and where the buses stopped. The MIT Civic Design Lab, the University of Nairobi, the Center for Sustainable Urban Development, and GroupShot helped to create maps using GPS, but the challenge that the MIT students tackled was keeping the maps accurate and current. Their solution used the MIT App Inventor to create *UMATI*, a crowd-sourced app, to track riders' routes and stops. They incentivize riders to collect data by offering them tokens (called MaTokens) that give discounts at local businesses. The following screenshots show the home screen and the Track Me screen:

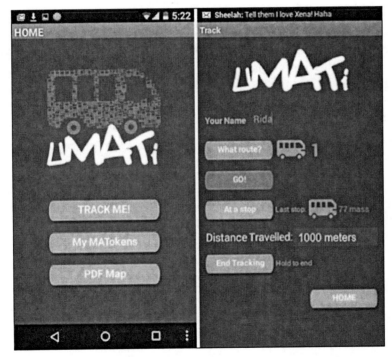

Components used: Button, Clock, Notifier, Image, Label, Location Sensor, ActivityStarter, FusiontablesControls, and Alignments

Ez School Bus Locator

Created by Arjun Santhosh Kumar, an eighth grader from Chennai, India, *Ez School Bus Locator* is a location-tracking app that allows schools, parents, and students to monitor the location of school buses through voice activation or a key tap. Students scan a QR code upon entering and exiting the bus, so parents can track their children's routes to and from school. Automated SMS messaging keeps parents informed. The following screenshots show the home screen and two views of a location-tracking screen:

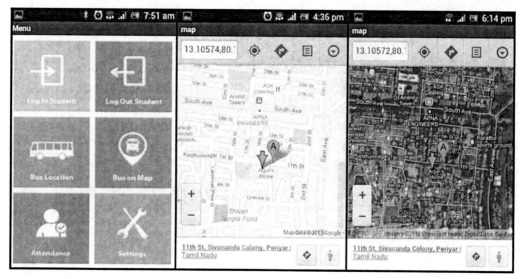

Components used: SMS messaging, GPS, map, QR Code, Button, Image, and Alignments

Youth Radio

This is an app that enables podcast listeners to rate radio shows and offer feedback.

Youth Radio is a non-profit organization based in Oakland, CA. Youth Radio programs empower young people to create media content by teaching them broadcast journalism and technology skills. Many of the podcasts that the students create are aired on National Public Radio across the United States. In an effort to interact with their listeners, develop relevant content, and get feedback, Youth Radio students created a mobile app with MIT App Inventor 2, enabling listeners to rate a radio show, add comments, and offer suggestions for future topics.

The following screenshots show the different ways that listeners can interact with Youth Radio:

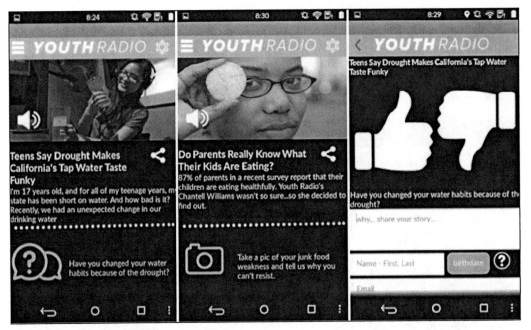

Components used: Button, Clock, Notifier, Image, Camera, TinyDB, Player, Sharing, Label, Location Sensor, FusiontablesControls, Alignments, and MediaStore

Rover 800 Remote

Rover 800 Remote app is an MIT App Inventor example of the Internet of Things. Paul Clements from the UK built a Bluetooth controller for his car that, with the help of microcontroller (sensor), can control the door locks, trunk release, fuel flap release, horn, and lights. It also remembers the car's address (if available), so if the cell phone housing the app is inadvertently locked in the car along with the keys, a text message sent from another phone can unlock the car. This app could be modified for a wide range of vehicles. The following screenshots show the home screen, the registration screen, and the overview screen:

Chapter 1

Components used: Bluetooth, List Picker, Button, Label, Image, and Alignments

Summary

While the bulk of this book centers on learning to code with MIT App Inventor, this particular chapter highlights the many other learning outcomes gained from engaging in the mobile app development process. Taking an app concept and building it out into an actual mobile app is both a concrete and a creative process. Attention to detail and iteration is vital for both code and design to work effectively and synergistically. Whether you're creating a game to play with your friend, an app to promote philanthropy involvement on campus, or an app to kickstart a recycling program in your neighborhood, the Design Thinking process is as much a part of app development as coding. Skills such as brainstorming, researching, interviewing, synthesizing, ideating, storyboarding, designing, troubleshooting, problem solving, and testing are not only integral to app building, but are also transferrable to other disciplines, helping to unlock creativity and flow in any endeavor.

Now that you've been introduced to MIT App Inventor and your new role as an app designer and developer, the next step will be to learn how to set up MIT App Inventor. Let's get rolling!

2
Setting Up MIT App Inventor 2

Now that you have been introduced to MIT App Inventor 2 and you have learned about your new role as an app developer and designer, let's get started with the technical setup! MIT App Inventor is a free web-based application that runs on a web browser and saves your projects on the cloud. The magical part about MIT App Inventor is that you can live test your app during each stage of development. In order to do this, you will need to set up connectivity that includes downloading software to connect your computer to your Android mobile device or between the onscreen emulator.

This chapter covers the following topics:

- System requirements
- Setting up a Google account
- Connecting your computer to your mobile device using wireless Internet (WiFi)
- Connecting your computer to your mobile device using a USB cable
- Connecting your computer to the onscreen emulator

The initial setup

To use MIT App Inventor, you will need a computer connected to the Internet, a web browser, a Google account, an Android phone or tablet (but if you don't have one, you can use the onscreen emulator), and a way to connect your computer to your phone (either with WiFi or a USB cable). Setting up MIT App Inventor for the first time can be a little daunting, but if you follow the steps based on your operating system and how you will be connecting (via WiFi, a USB cable, or an emulator), it can be a straightforward process. And remember, once you complete the technical setup, you can start building mobile apps!

System requirements

In this section, we will cover the recommended software requirements that your system (PC, browser, and Android device) must have in order to run MIT App Inventor without any hassles.

Computer and operating system requirements:

- **Macintosh (with an Intel processor)**: Mac OS X 10.5 or higher
- **Windows**: Windows XP, Windows Vista, Windows 7, Windows 8, or Windows 10
- **GNU/Linux**: Ubuntu 8 or higher, or Debian 5 or higher (note: GNU/Linux IDE is only supported for WiFi connections between computers and Android devices)

Browser requirements:

- Mozilla Firefox 3.6 or higher (if you are using Firefox and have the NoScript extension installed, you will have to disable it by turning the extension off)
- Apple Safari 5.0 or higher
- Google Chrome 4.0 or higher
- Note: Microsoft Internet Explorer is not supported

Android device (phone or tablet) requirements:

- Android Operating System 2.3 (Gingerbread) or higher

Signing up a Google account

If you already have a Google Account (or a Google Gmail account), please skip to the section: *Logging into MIT App Inventor.*

The login authentication and storage for MIT App Inventor projects are linked to a Google account. Thus, you need to set one up. It is free! You will also need this Google account when you are ready to upload your completed apps onto the Google Play marketplace. There is an option to create an online profile, which you can make public or private.

> You can sign up for a Google account with or without creating a Gmail e-mail account. For example, some school systems use *Google for Education* with Google accounts, but students do not have Gmail addresses.

The minimum age to set up a Google account in the Netherlands is 16, in Spain and South Korea, it is 14, and in the US and all the other countries, it is 13.

Sign up for a Google account at https://accounts.google.com/signup. The form asks you to create a username and password; you will need these to use MIT App Inventor. While there is a field to enter a mobile phone number, it is not a required field. However, you will need to enter an e-mail address to complete the setup. If you don't have an e-mail ID, please ask a parent, guardian, or teacher to fill one in. It is used for security purposes, for example, to help recover a forgotten password.

Logging in to MIT App Inventor

Once you have set up your Google account, you can log into MIT App Inventor for the first time at http://ai2.appinventor.mit.edu/ (or by clicking the **Create Apps!** button on the home page http://appinventor.mit.edu/). Either method directs you to the Google Sign-in screen.

If you are not signed into your Google account, a login screen will appear, asking for your username and password. If you are already signed into your Google account from a previous session, you will see the following message:

The application MIT App Inventor Version 2 is requesting permission to access your Google Account. Please select an account that you would like to use.

Your Google account will appear with a radio button next to it. Click on the **Allow** button or you can choose another account, if you have one. The choices will look as follows:

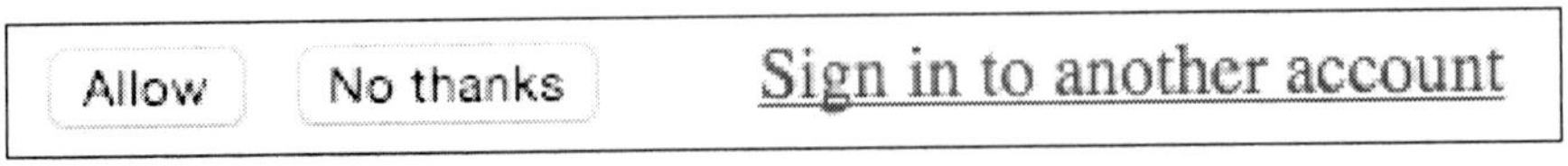

Allow	No thanks	Sign in to another account

Once signed in, you will be directed back to MIT App Inventor, where new users will need to agree to the MIT App Inventor privacy policy and terms of use by clicking on the button at the bottom of the page, which will look as follows:

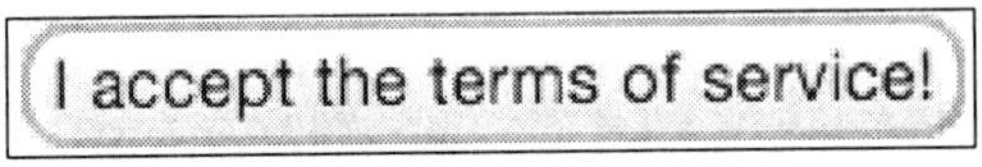

I accept the terms of service!

Next, you will be taken to the projects page. A pop-up window will ask you to take a short survey. The information you provide is confidential and it will assist with research and help the MIT App Inventor team to improve its service for users around the world. The survey is optional; click on one of the three options, as shown in the following screenshot:

Welcome to MIT App Inventor!

Please fill out a short voluntary survey so that we can learn more about our users and improve MIT App Inventor.

Take Survey Now	Take Survey Later	Never Take Survey

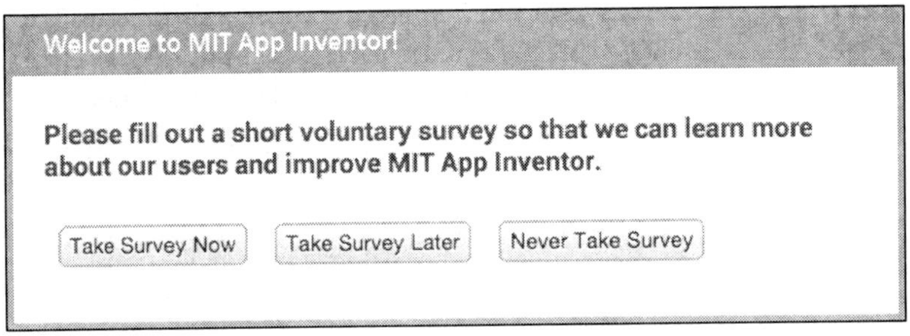

Then, you will see a pop-up window that looks similar to the following screenshot:

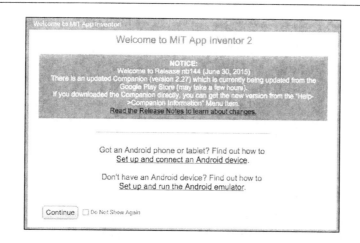

This type of information windows will appear regularly when logging into the MIT App Inventor (unless you opt out by clicking on the **Do Not Show Again** checkbox) to give you latest information from our developers about updates and releases. They also provide links to help you get connected. Be sure to read these when they appear, so you can get the relevant information on MIT App Inventor updates. Then, click on the **Continue** button.

To create your first MIT App Inventor project, click on the **Start new project** button in the upper-left corner of the screen, as shown in the following screenshot:

A pop-up window (as shown in the following screenshot) will ask you to name your project. No spaces are allowed in project names:

Once you type a name, click on the **OK** button. The project you just named will exist under both **Projects** and **My Projects** in the top menu bar (as shown in the following screenshot):

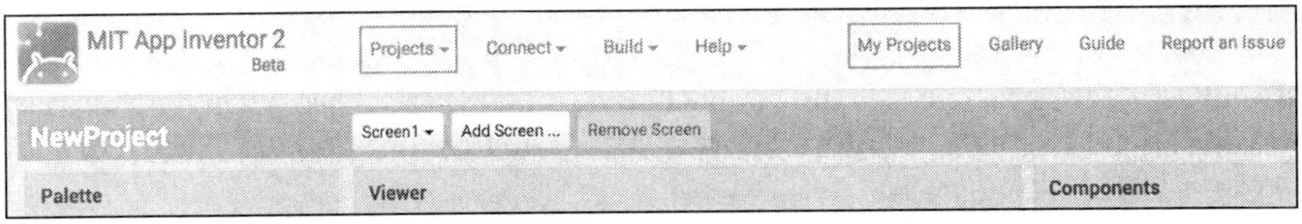

Congratulations! You are now in the Designer window (as shown in the following screenshot); it is the **Graphical User Interface (GUI)** where you will create the look and feel of your app:

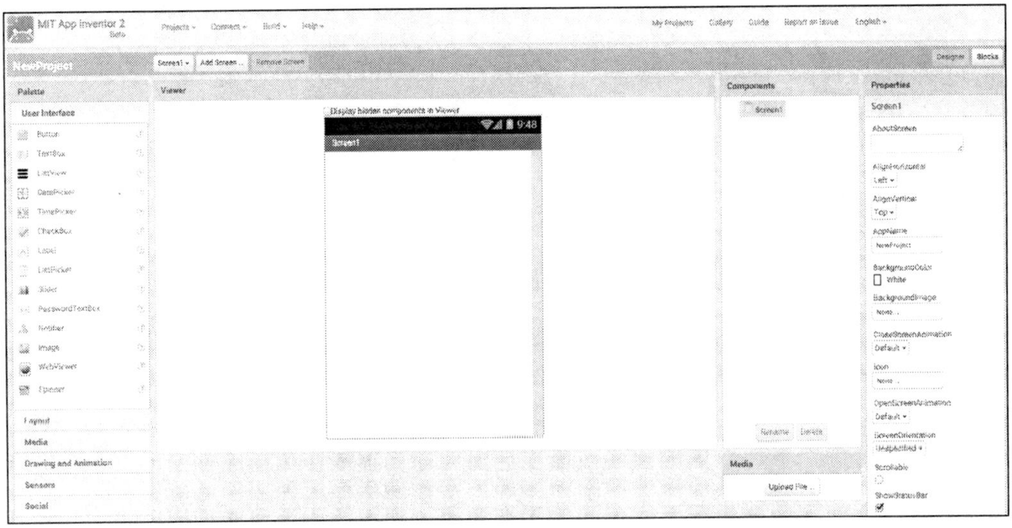

You are now ready to establish connectivity!

If at any point during the connectivity setup process, you need additional help, click on **Guide** in the upper-right corner of the top menu bar of the Designer window (as shown in the following screenshot):

MIT App Inventor 2 Beta	Projects ▾ Connect ▾ Build ▾ Help ▾		My Projects Gallery	Guide	Report an Issue
NewProject	Screen1 ▾ Add Screen ... Remove Screen				
Palette	Viewer			Components	

Connectivity setup

This first set of instructions is for all the users with an Android mobile device regardless of how you will be connecting this device to your computer (WiFi or USB cable) and regardless of your computer's operating system (Mac, Windows, or GNU/Linux). If you will be using the onscreen emulator, skip to section: *Connecting the emulator or connecting using a USB Cable*.

Now that you have completed the initial setup to create a project in MIT App Inventor, you are almost ready to create apps. But first, you need to connect your computer to your Android mobile device so that you can see your app take shape as you build it. To do this, you will need the free AI2 Companion App.

Downloading the AI2 Companion app

There are two ways you can get the AI2 Companion app onto your Android device: through the Google Play Store or through direct download. Following are instructions for both methods:

- **Google Play (recommended for automatic updates)**: If your device has a QR code reader app installed, you can scan this QR code (see the following image). It will take you to the Google Play Store where you can download the AI2 Companion app to your device. (If you don't have a QR code reader, you can find one for free by doing a search in the Google Play Store.)

Alternatively, you can access the Google Play Store to download the AI2 Companion app by typing the following URL in a web browser on your device:

`https://play.google.com/store/apps/details?id=edu.mit.appinventor.aicompanion3`

- **Direct APK download (requires manual updates)**: If for some reason you cannot access the Google Play Store, you can download the app directly on your phone by scanning this QR code (see the following image):

Alternatively, you can download the app by typing the following URL in a web browser on your device: `http://appinv.us/companion`.

Note that when downloading the app directly (also known as side-loading), you will need to do as follows:

1. Change your device's settings to allow the installation of apps from unknown sources. To find this setting on versions of Android prior to 4.0, go to **Settings | Applications** and then check the box next to **Unknown Sources**. For devices running Android 4.0 or later, go to **Settings | Security** or **Settings | Security & Screen Lock** and then check the box next to **Unknown Sources** and confirm your choice.

2. Manually update the MIT AI2 Companion app. Since you will not receive automatic updates from the Google Play Store, whenever you log in to App Inventor and see an information window popup indicating that the MIT AI2 Companion app has been upgraded, you will need to install the new version by repeating the direct downloading (side-loading) steps. But first, you must uninstall the previous version of the MIT AI2 Companion app. To uninstall, locate the MIT AI2 Companion app's icon on your phone and tap and hold it until you see a message with an uninstall option. Click on **uninstall**.

Connecting your computer and Android device with WiFi

These instructions are for Android device users, who will be connecting to their computer via wireless Internet (WiFi).

The fun part about building apps with the MIT App Inventor is live testing, that is, seeing your progress appear on your mobile device in real time. For the IDE to function properly and automatically update your app on your device; you must ensure that your computer (running MIT App Inventor) and your Android device (running the AI2 Companion app) **are connected to the same WiFi network**. Please ensure that this is the case before you continue.

On your computer, in the Designer window, click on the top menu item, **Connect**, and choose **AI Companion** from the drop-down list, as shown in the following screenshot:

A pop-up window with a QR code and a six-character code will appear on your computer screen.

On your mobile device, launch the AI2 Companion by clicking on the app's icon. A screen will appear with the following options: type in the six-character code or scan QR code:

- **To connect with QR code**: Click on the blue button on your mobile device that says **scan QR code**. This will launch the QR code reader in the AI2 Companion app. Hold the mobile device up to the QR code on the computer screen to automatically scan.

- **To connect with six-character code**: Simply type in the six-character code shown on your computer screen into the white text box on your mobile device that says **Six Character Code** (do not click return or enter on your keyboard). Then, click on the orange button **connect with code**.

The following screenshot summarizes the connectivity steps:

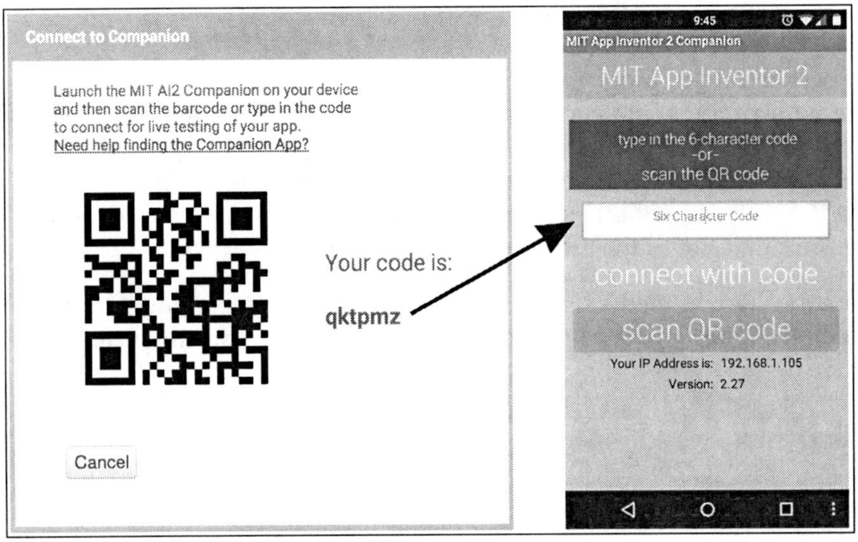

The code on your computer and your mobile device

Within a few seconds, you will see **Screen1** from the designer window appear on your mobile device.

If not, try the following troubleshooting options:

- Your device may not be connected to WiFi. Make sure you see an IP address at the bottom of the AI2 Companion app screen on your phone or tablet (see the preceding screenshot).

- Your mobile device and computer may not be connected to the same WiFi network.

Connecting the emulator or connecting using a USB cable

These instructions (Steps1-4) are for emulator users or for those connecting a computer to a mobile device via USB cable.

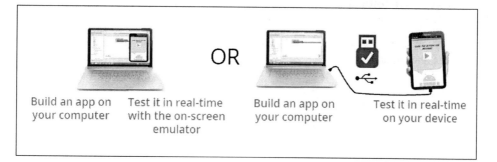

If you do not have a mobile device, don't worry; you can still test the apps you build with MIT App Inventor by using the onscreen emulator. It simulates an Android mobile device (although there are some functions that cannot be tested, such as the accelerometer). You can use the emulator to share apps with others, even through the Google Play Store. Many people build apps this way.

On the other hand, you may have an Android device, but your school or organization may have firewalls preventing the use of WiFi. In this case, you can still use live testing by connecting your computer to your mobile device using a USB cable.

The same software and setup is needed whether you are connecting to the emulator or connecting your mobile device via a USB cable.

Step 1 – installing the App Inventor setup software

Follow the instructions for your computer's operating system.

Installing the App Inventor setup software for Mac OS X

Use the following steps to install the App Inventor setup software on your Mac OS X:

1. Download the installer via `http://appinv.us/aisetup_mac`.

2. Double-click on the downloaded file (most probably located in the `Downloads` folder) to start the installer `AppInventor_Setup_v_X.X.dmg` (where `X.X` is the version number).

3. Depending on your settings, you may see a pop-up window informing you that the file cannot be opened (as shown in the following screenshot):

4. If the MIT App Inventor setup software cannot be opened, go to **System Preferences | Security & Privacy | General** and click on the **Open Anyway** button, as shown in the following screenshot:

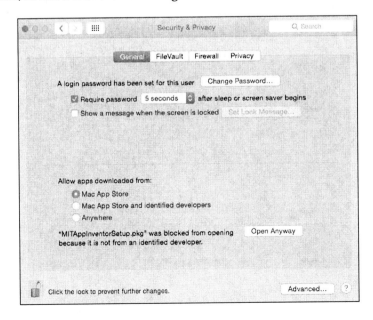

5. If your settings are locked, you may have to enter your administrator password in order to make changes.

6. You will see a welcome message, as shown in the following screenshot. Then, click on the **Continue** button.

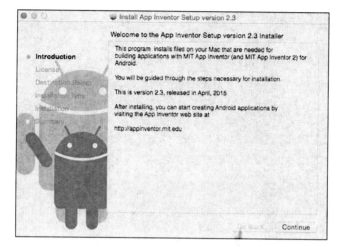

7. Read and accept the software license agreement (not shown).

On the **Standard Install** screen (as shown in the following screenshot), click on **Install**:

Note: Don't change the install location.

8. Enter your computer's password to confirm that you want to install the software (not shown). Click on **Ok**.

9. The installer confirms that the App Inventor Setup package was installed (as shown in the following screenshot):

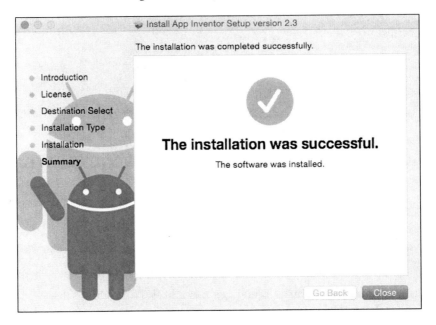

Depending on how you will be connecting your computer to your device, Mac users can proceed to *Step 3 – opening a project and connecting to the emulator or Step 4 - setting up your device with a USB cable*.

Installing the App Inventor setup software for Windows

This set of instructions consists of *part A* and *part B*.

Software installation – part A

1. Type the following URL in a web browser on your computer to download the installer: http://appinv.us/aisetup_windows.

2. Locate the MIT_App_Inventor_Tools_2.3.0_win_setup.exe (~80 MB) file in your Downloads folder or on your desktop. The location of the downloaded file on your computer will depend on how your browser is configured.

3. Open the file by double-clicking on it.

4. You may be asked if you want to allow a program from an unknown publisher to make changes to this computer (as shown in the following screenshot). Then, click on the **Run** button.

5. You will see a **Welcome to the MIT App Inventor Tools 2.3.0 Setup** window (as shown in the following screenshot). Then, click on the **Next** button.

6. Read and accept the software license agreement (as shown in the following screenshot). Then, click on the **I Agree** button.

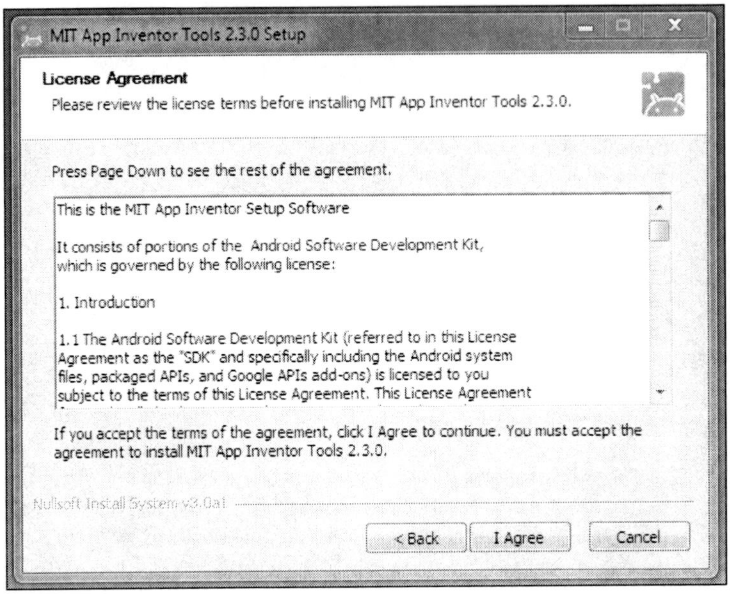

7. Choose among the installation options. You can select whether you want to install the setup tools for all users or a single user. Note that you will need administrative privileges if you choose all users (as shown in the following screenshot). Then, click on the **Next** button.

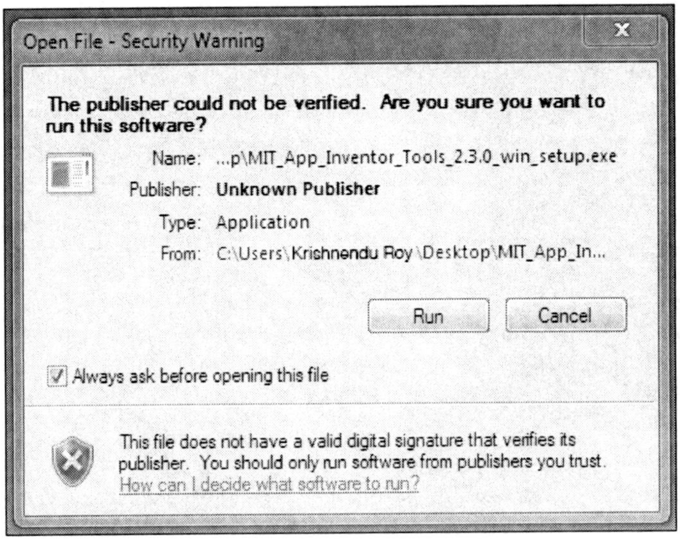

8. **Install Location** is set to the default location depending on whether you are running a 32-bit or 64-bit machine as a single user or for all users (as shown in the following screenshot). Then, click on the **Next** button.

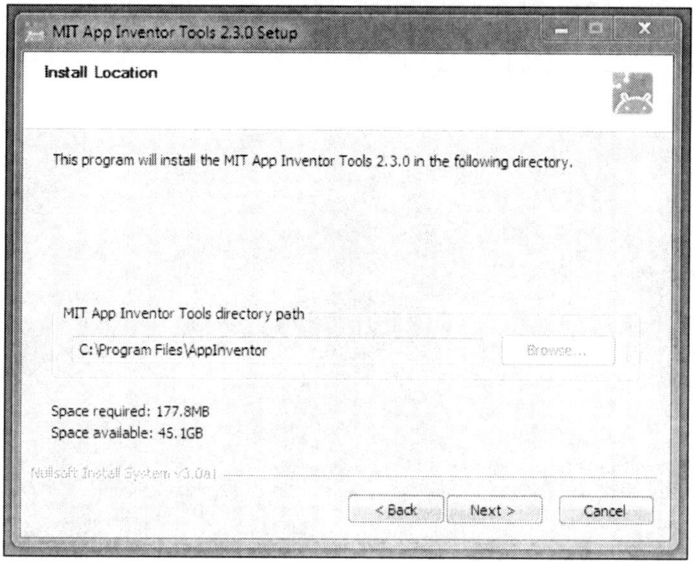

9. Choose installation components. By default the installer will install the setup tools but gives you the option to add a desktop icon (as shown in the following screenshot). Then, click on the **Next** button.

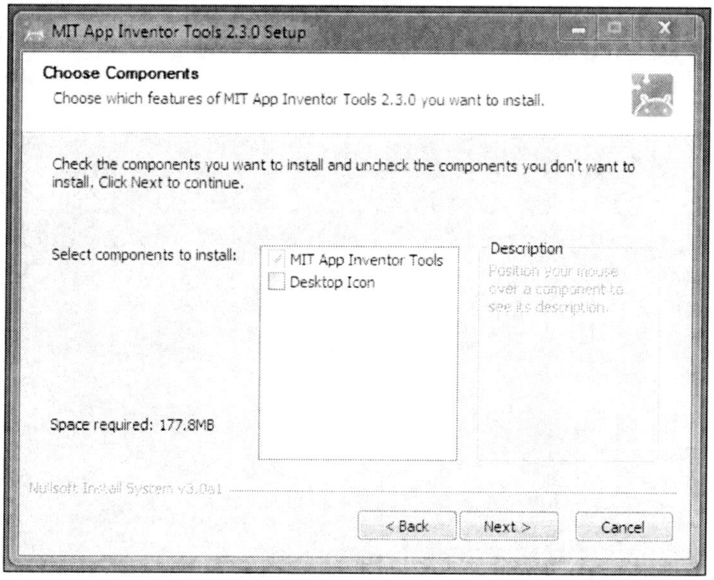

10. Choose a **Start Menu** folder. By default, it is set to **MIT App Inventor Tools** (as shown in the following screenshot). Then, click on the **Install** button.

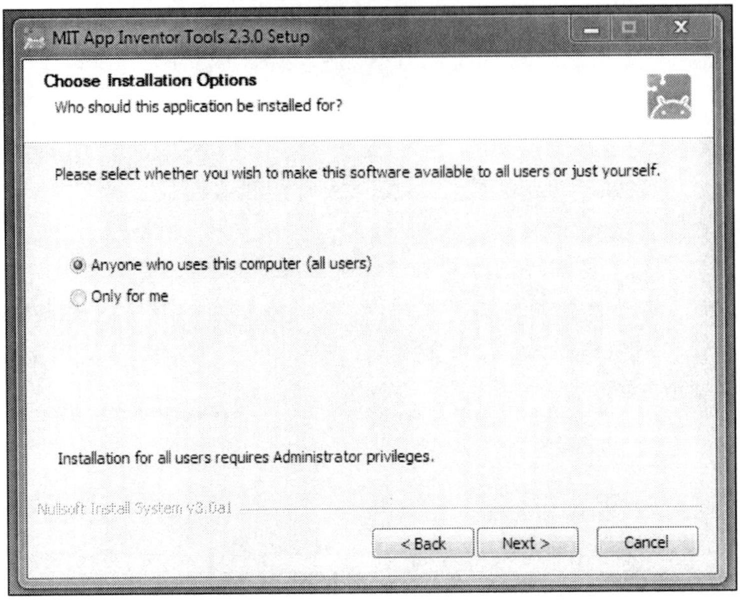

11. You will now see a progress bar that shows which files are being installed along with the status (the percentage of completion) of the installation. Wait for a few minutes for this process to finish.

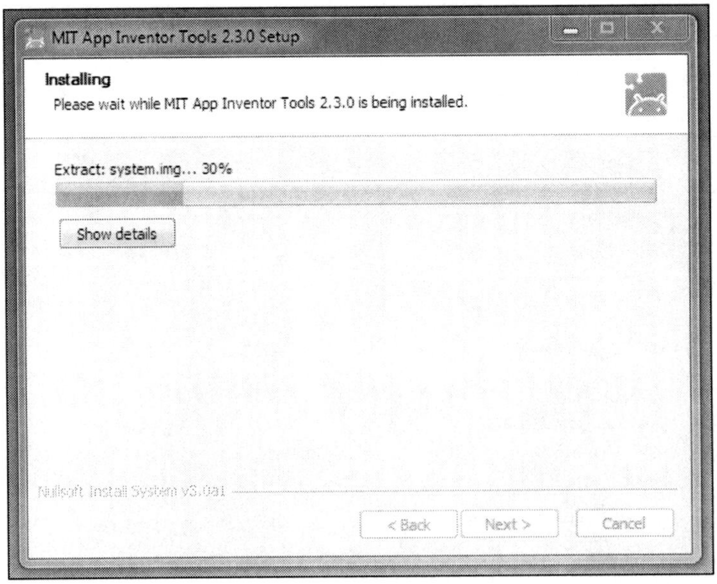

12. After the MIT App Inventor Tools is installed, the last screen will by default automatically launch the `aiStarter` program for you. Deselect this option if you don't want it to be started at this point (as shown in the following screenshot). Click on **Finish**.

Driver installation – part B

If you choose to connect your Android device using a USB cable to a Windows machine, then you will need to install special Windows driver software. Different devices may require different drivers. Manufacturers often create and supply the drivers. You may need to search the Web to find the appropriate driver for your Android device.

 More information and installation instructions can be found at `http://developer.android.com/sdk/win-usb.html` and `http://appinventor.mit.edu/explore/content/windows-drivers.html`.

Windows users, proceed to Step 2- Launch aiStarter.

Installing the App Inventor setup software for GNU/Linux

You'll need `sudo` (`super-user do`) privileges to do the installation.

Note that the setup programs are 32-bit software. If you have a 64-bit system, you may need to install libraries that let your machine run 32-bit software. One way to do this is to run the following command:

```
> sudo apt-get install lib32z1
```

But, this might not work on all the GNU/Linux distributions, and you may need to do some investigation on this topic for your particular system.

Instructions for systems that can install Debian packages (for example Debian or Ubuntu)

1. Download the file by typing the following URL in a web browser on your computer: http://commondatastorage.googleapis.com/ appinventordownloads/appinventor2-setup_1.1_all.deb. The Debian file name is appinventor2-setup_1.1_all.deb. The location of the downloaded file on your computer depends on how your browser is configured. Typically, it will go into your Downloads folder.

2. If your system can install packages simply by clicking on the package file, then do so.

3. If your system doesn't support clickable package installers, then navigate to the directory where the file is located and run the following command:

    ```
    > sudo dpkg --install appinventor2-setup_1.1_all.deb
    ```

4. With either method, you might need to ensure that the Debian file and the directory it's located in are world-readable and world-executable. On some systems, sudo does not have default privileges to read and execute all the files. The software will be installed under /usr/google/appinventor.

5. You might also need to configure your system to detect your device. See the Android developer instructions at the following link: http://developer. android.com/guide/developing/device.html#setting-up. Find the instructions under **(#3) Set up your system to detect your device**. Go to the third bullet starting with **If you're developing on Ubuntu Linux...**.

Instructions for other GNU/Linux systems

1. Download the file from the following link: http://commondatastorage. googleapis.com/appinventordownloads/appinventor2-setup_1.1.tar. gz. The file is named appinventor2-setup_1.1.tar.gz and it is a GZIP compressed tar file. The location of the downloaded file on your computer will depend on how your browser is configured. Typically, it will go into your Downloads folder.

2. Install the files by first decompressing the file and then copying the `appinventor` directory and its contents to the location `/usr/google/appinventor` using a method appropriate for your operating system.

GNU/Linux users proceed to the next step.

Step 2 – launch aiStarter

This step is for Windows and GNU/Linux users connecting with the emulator or with a USB cable. Mac users connecting with the emulator can skip to *Step 3 – opening a project and connecting to the emulator*. Mac users connecting with a USB cable can skip to *Step 4 – setting up your device with a USB cable*.

Starting aiStarter

The aiStarter program manages communication between the web browser and the Android device (note that on the Mac platform, the aiStarter program automatically starts at login). Whenever you log in to use MIT App Inventor with the emulator or a USB cable on a GNU/Linux or Windows machine, you will need to start the aiStarter program.

GNU/Linux users can do this with the following command:

```
> /usr/google/appinventor/commands-for-Appinventor/aiStarter &
```

Windows users can locate the aiStarter program from **Start Menu** or by double-clicking on the aiStarter shortcut located on the desktop if you installed it during the MIT App Inventor Setup tools installation process.

For convenience, you may want to arrange for this command to run automatically whenever you log in or when the system starts. The precise way to do this depends on which GNU/Linux distribution you are using. If this is unfamiliar to you, please consult the documentation that comes with your distribution.

Proceed to the next step.

Step 3 – opening a project and connecting to the emulator

This step is for all users connecting with the emulator regardless of the operating system. All the users connecting with a USB can skip to *Step 4 – setting up your device with a USB cable*.

Since you have already created your first project and named it, we now will connect the emulator to display it.

On your computer, in the designer window, click on **Connect** located at the top menu bar and choose **Emulator** from the drop-down list.

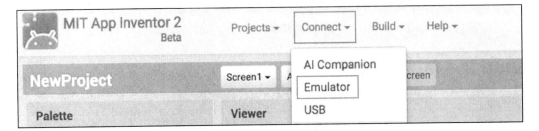

A popup will inform you that the emulator is connecting. This can take a few minutes.

The emulator will initially appear with an empty black screen (**#1**). Wait until the emulator is ready with a colored screen background (**#2**). After the background appears, you should continue waiting until the emulator has finished preparing its SD card; there will be a notice at the top of the phone screen while the card is being prepared (**#3**). When connected, the emulator will launch and display the app you, open in MIT App Inventor (**#4** is empty, because for now, the new project is empty).

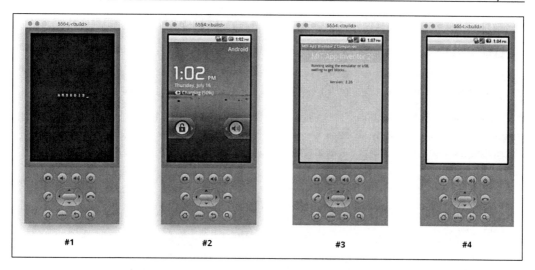

Step 4 – setting up your device with a USB cable

This step is for all users connecting with a USB cable regardless of the operating system.

On your Android device, go to **Settings | Developer options**, turn it on, and ensure that **USB debugging** is turned on.

On most devices running Android 3.2 or older, you can find this option under **Settings | Applications | Development**.

On Android 4.0 and newer, you can find it in **Settings | Developer options**.

> On Android 4.2 and newer, **Developer options** is hidden by default. To make it available, go to **Settings | About phone | Build number** and tap on **Build number** seven times. Return to the previous screen, go to **Settings | Developer options | USB debugging** and tap on it to enable it (on some devices, it may be listed as **Android debugging**).

Step 5 – connecting your computer and device (authenticating if necessary)

These instructions continue from *Step 4 – setting up your device with a USB cable* for all users connecting with a USB cable regardless of the operating system.

Connect your Android device to the computer using a USB cable. Ensure that the device connects as a **mass storage device** (not as a **media device**) and that it is not mounted as a drive on your computer.

> Note that if it is mounted, you can find it un-mount the device, using the following instructions, but make sure your device is connected to the computer via the USB cable.

There are three ways to un-mount any drive(s) that were mounted when you connected your Android device by USB cable. They are as follows:

- Right-click to eject it
- Click on it and drag it to the trash
- Use **Finder** (on Mac) or **My Computer** (on Windows) and click on the arrow next to the name

The first time you connect your Android device (4.2.2 and newer) to the computer, a pop-up screen will appear on your device with the message: **Allow USB Debugging?** Press **OK**. This will authenticate the computer to the device, allowing the computer to communicate with it. You'll need to do this for each computer you want to connect to the device, but only once per computer.

Step 6 – testing the connection

These instructions continue from *Step 5 – connecting your computer and device (authenticating if necessary)* for all users connecting with a USB cable regardless of the operating system.

With your mobile device still connected to your computer, go to `http://appinventor.mit.edu/test` (this will open in a new tab on your browser) and see whether you have gotten a confirmation that your computer can detect the device. If the test fails, go to `http://appinventor.mit.edu/explore/ai2/connection-help.html` and look at USB help for your computer (Windows or Mac). You won't be able to use App Inventor with a USB cable until you resolve the connection issue.

Summary

As you may have discovered, establishing connectivity from the MIT App Inventor web application on your computer to an Android mobile device or onscreen emulator takes some time and patience. But we guarantee it is worth the effort. As you start building an app and seeing its live development on your mobile device (or emulator), it is not only exciting and satisfying, but necessary and helpful for designing, troubleshooting, and testing. If you get stuck, you can always visit the support pages on the MIT App Inventor website (`http://appinventor.mit.edu/`) or ask for help in the community forum. Now that the technical setup is over, the fun is about to begin! Let's learn how to make mobile apps with the MIT App Inventor!

3
Navigating the App Inventor Platform

Now that you have created a new project and set up connectivity, you are ready to begin learning how to make mobile apps! This chapter will provide a step-by-step guide to navigate the App Inventor web application through the process of building a game app called Fling. You will be using:

- The Projects View
- The Designer (a graphical user interface)
    - ° Palette
    - ° Viewer
    - ° Components
    - ° Properties
- The Blocks Editor (a visual programming language)
- The Integrated Development Environment (IDE)

The projects view

In *Chapter 2, Setting Up MIT App Inventor 2*, you logged into App Inventor for the first time, created a new project, and named it, so at the moment, you only have one App Inventor project. Once you start building more apps, all of the projects associated with your Google Account will be listed under My Projects. Every time you log into App Inventor, the platform will automatically open the most recent project that you worked on. To pick a different project, click on **My Projects** in the top menu bar, or to start a new project, click on **Start new project** in the upper left corner.

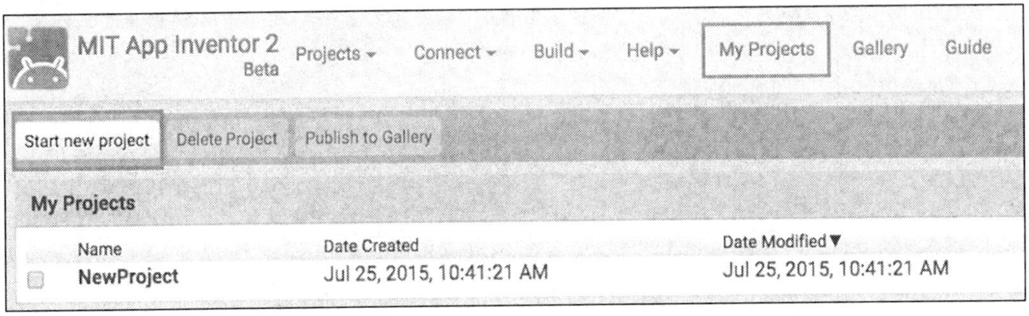

Creating a new project

We're going to build a game in this chapter. It will be similar to Pong, but instead of a paddle, you will use your finger to fling the ball. Let's create a new project called `Fling`. Note that project names containing no spaces must start with a letter. Use only letters, underscores, and numbers. Click on **Start new project** in the upper-left corner of the screen. A pop-up window will appear, as shown in the following screenshot. Type in the word **Fling**. Once you click on **OK**, you will be taken into the Designer.

If you happen to have a previous project open in the Designer, you can still start a new project in this view by clicking on **Start new project** listed under **Projects** in the top menu bar, as shown in the following screenshot:

The Designer

When you open a project or start a new project, App Inventor will take you to the Designer. This window is a graphical editor where you can create the look and feel of your mobile app by choosing components (buttons, labels, images, and so on), layouts (horizontal/vertical alignments), colors, fonts, and more. The next screenshot is a layout of the Designer (with some helpful navigation hints):

The name of the open project is displayed in the upper-left corner. In the upper-right corner, you will see toggle buttons for the **Designer** and **Blocks** Editor (the **Designer** button is disabled at the moment, since we are currently in the Designer view). The Designer consists of five panels, which are explained as follows.

Palette

The **Palette** (found in the left-hand column of the previous Designer image) contains drawers that hold sets of tools called **Components**. Drawers group **Components** by type such as **User Interface, Layout, Media, Drawing and Animation, Sensors, Social, Storage, Connectivity,** and **LEGO MINDSTORMS**. It will take a little bit of time to remember which drawer houses which Components and what functions they have. More on Components later!

Viewer

The **Viewer** (found in the middle of the preceding Designer image) is the white workspace in the middle of the Designer window. When you first create a project, the default workspace name is **Screen1**. You cannot change the name of Screen1, although you can change the title of the screen name. This can be done in the **Properties** panel (as follows). The new screen name will be displayed in the Viewer and be seen by app users. Later, you may want to add more screens to your app and you can rename the subsequent screens. To build your app, you will drag Components from the Palette drawers onto the Viewer. We will be using visual components in our Fling app, so these will remain visible when dragged into the Viewer. In the subsequent chapters, we will demonstrate the use of non-visible components, which will not remain in the Viewer when added. Instead, they will be housed underneath the Viewer.

Components

Components are the tools located in the **Palette** drawers on the left-hand side of the Designer window (we will demonstrate what different components do once we start building apps). Once Components are dragged into the Viewer, they will also appear in the Components panel (found in the middle right of the Designer image). The Components panel lists Components and organizes them by screens. You can collapse and expand the screen Component contents for convenience. Components are listed in columns so that it is easy to see whether they exist on their own or within other Components.

To illustrate that some Components are inside other Components, the Components panel will display them in a nested (indented) list. Note that when you click on a Component in the Viewer, it will be highlighted in both the Viewer and the Components panel and display editable options in the **Properties** panel (described in the following section). And conversely, if you click on a Component in the Components panel, it will also be highlighted in the Viewer. Once a Component is clicked and it becomes active, you can either rename or delete it by clicking the **Rename** or **Delete** button or you can view or edit its settings in the Properties panel.

Properties

The **Properties** panel (found in the right-hand side column of the preceding Designer image) displays a set of configurable settings (such as size, color, and alignments) for each **Screen** and **Component** added to the **Viewer**. In the subsequent chapters, you will be adding more and more Components (and Screens), so make certain that the correct item is highlighted before you change its settings. The name of the active Component (or Screen) appears at the top of the Properties pane (in the earlier Designer screenshot, the active **Property** is **Screen1** as indicated at the top of the **Properties** panel).

Media

The **Media** panel is located underneath the Components panel (see the Designer screenshot). This feature enables you to upload images, sound files, or other media files from your computer to your project. If you find a *creative commons* (freely shared, uncopyrighted) photo online that you'd like to use in your app, you must first download it and then click on the **Upload** File button in the media panel (you cannot download an image from the Internet directly into the App Inventor). Once the file is uploaded, it will be listed in both the **Media** panel and the Properties panel (to delete media files, click on the media file name and a popup will appear to delete the file). Note that even though the media files can also be added to the Properties panel, they cannot be deleted from the Properties panel. How to use an image, sound, or video file in your app will be explained in the future chapters.

Creating a game app

You've already logged into App Inventor with your Google Account, created a new project, named it Fling, and learned how to navigate the Designer screen. It's time to create your first mobile app!

> Since this is a tutorial, we will explain the way to play our game. But, if you were starting from scratch to create your own game, you would want to make sure that you've put in the time, effort, and energy to figure out what you want it to do and what you want it to look like. We outlined the design process for mobile app creation in *Chapter 1, Unleashing Creativity with MIT App Inventor 2*. This may be a good time to review it.

The object of the Fling game app is to fling a moving ball with your finger to prevent it from hitting the bottom edge of the screen and ending the game. When the Play button is clicked, the ball will start moving from top to bottom. If it hits the bottom edge of the screen before the user flings it away, the game will stop and a **Game Over** notice will appear on the screen. The **Reset** button resets the ball to the top of the screen and the **Play** button starts another round. In this game, you will learn to design the user interface using these Components: a ball, a canvas (the game board), a horizontal layout, buttons, and a label. You will learn to program:

- An animated object (ball) that moves randomly
- Conditions where the ball will respond to a screen touch
- An end-game mechanism when the ball touches the bottom of the screen
- A game over display when the game ends
- A button that starts the game by moving the ball downward
- A button that resets the game by repositioning the ball at the top of the screen and erases the "game over" display

As you build your app, you will see your progress unfold on your mobile device or emulator in real time using the **IDE (Integrated Development Environment)**. Let's get started!

Creating the UI in designer

The first thing you will notice in a new project is that Screen1 automatically exists in the Viewer. As shown in the following screenshot, the name Screen1 appears in three places: in the **Viewer**, the **Components** panel, and the Properties panel. Note that this is also true for any component added to the Viewer. When a component is highlighted (as shown with a light green box) in the Components panel, you will see the corresponding properties for it in the Properties panel. While the name Screen1 is not editable, the properties associated with Screen1 are such as the title, although we won't be changing the Screen1 Properties in Fling.

Chapter 3

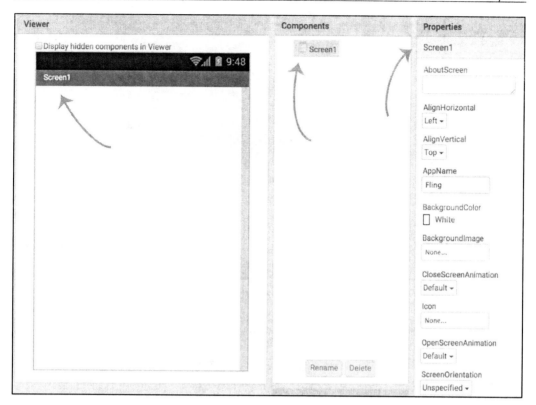

To create a game interface for the Fling app, we will:

1. Add the canvas Component to **Screen1**.
2. Click on the Palette drawer: **Drawing and Animation**. It will open to reveal three components: **Canvas**, **ImageSprite**, and **Ball**.

3. Click on **Canvas** and drag it to the **Viewer**, as shown in the following screenshot:

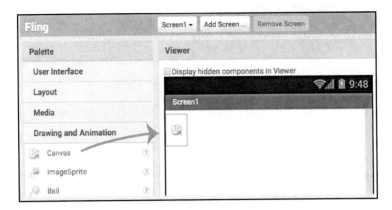

Your Designer window will look like the following screenshot. The Canvas component will automatically be named **Canvas1** in the Components panel. If you were to add another Canvas, it would automatically be named Canvas2. It is possible to rename Canvas1, although we are not going to for this tutorial, since it is aptly named. You can see that it is active (as it is highlighted with a light green box) in both the **Viewer** and the **Components** panel. Being active means that you are able to see and edit its properties in the **Properties** panel.

The Canvas is going to hold our Ball component, so we need to make it fill the whole screen not just a tiny part of the screen like it is now. To change the size of the Canvas, go to the **Properties** panel and click on the white text box below the **Height** element (currently filled with the word Automatic). A pop-up box will offer choices with radio buttons, as shown in the following screenshot. Click on the radio button next to **Fill Parent**. Click on the **OK** button.

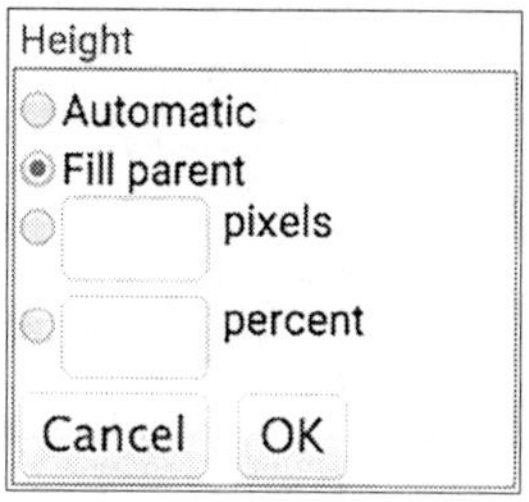

Repeat these steps for the **Width**. You will see that the Canvas now fills the entire Viewer. Next we will change the color. At the top of the **Properties** panel, click on the word **White** underneath **BackgroundColor**. A drop-down list of colors will appear (not shown); select **Gray**. The Designer window should now look like the following screenshot with the gray canvas filling up the entire Viewer.

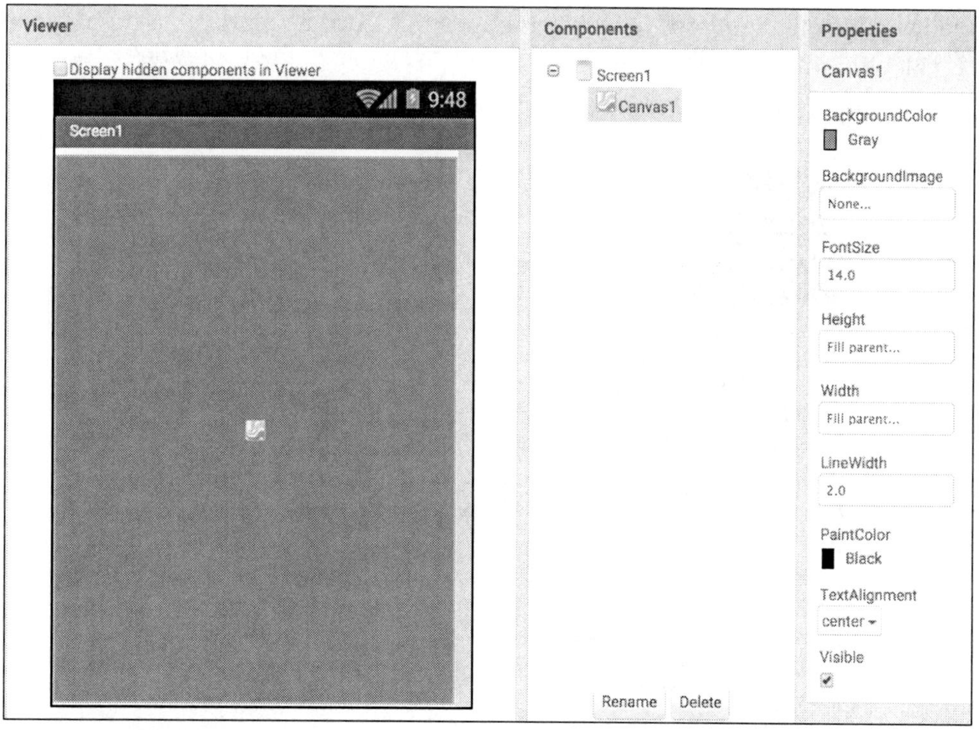

Next, we will add a ball. Go back to the **Drawing and Animation** Capitalize Palette drawer, click on **Ball**, and drag it to the **Canvas** in the Viewer, as shown in the following screenshot:

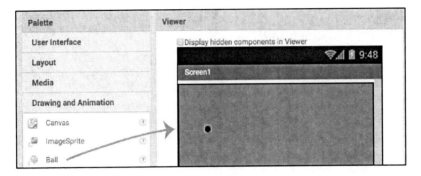

The Ball will end up on the Canvas wherever you drop it. It is named Ball1 in the Components panel. Notice how Ball1 appears nested (indented) in the Components panel list. This is because you placed it within another component, the Canvas1.

You can position the ball's starting location, size, and color in the Properties panel. Since **Ball1** is already active, you can begin editing the options in the **Properties** panel. Change the settings to match those shown in the following screenshot. We will actually end up changing the ball's starting position once we start programming, but this is just to get you familiar with the features available in the Properties panel.

Next, you will create a menu bar at the bottom of the screen. Since we want the buttons to be horizontal across the bottom of the screen, we will open the **Layout** palette drawer. Drag **HorizontalArrangement** to the bottom of the **Viewer** so that it sits underneath the **Canvas** and not inside the **Canvas**. It should look like the following screenshot:

You will know you did this correctly by looking at the Components panel. HorizontalArrangement should be listed in the same column under Canvas1 and not be indented like Ball1. If it is indented, it means that the HorizontalArrangement Component is inside the Canvas. We don't want that so, if it is, go to the **Viewer** and drag the **HorizontalArrangement** component out of the **Canvas** and position it below the **Canvas**. To shrink the size of **HorizontalArrangement**, edit the **Height** and **Width** options in the **Properties** panel to match the ones below. There are two ways to check whether you did this correctly. In the Viewer, HorizontalArrangement will create white space below the gray Canvas, as shown in the preceding screenshot. And, in the Components panel, HorizontalArrangement will align with Canvas1, as shown in the following screenshot. If you accidentally did this incorrectly and dropped HorizontalArrangement inside the Canvas, there would be no white space below the gray Canvas in the Viewer and the HorizontalArrangement component would be indented and aligned directly under Ball1.

To resize **HorizontalArrangement**, edit the **Height** and **Width** options in the **Properties** panel to match the following screenshot:

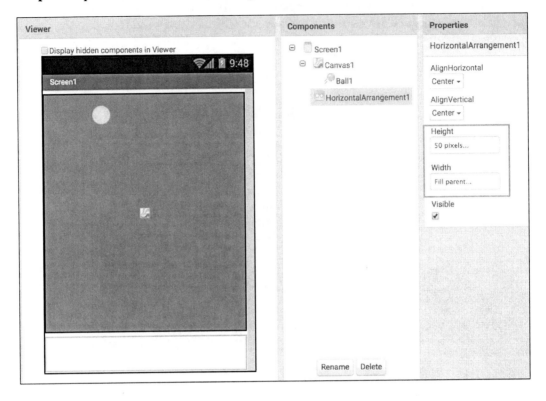

Next, drag a **Button** from the **User Interface** palette drawer into the **HorizontalArrangement** component at the bottom of **Screen1**. The button will say **Text for Button1**, as shown in the following screenshot:

You can verify that you did this correctly by seeing whether your screen matches the **Viewer** in the preceding screenshot. Also, in the **Components** panel, you will see that **Button1** will be nested underneath **HorizontalArrangement** and will therefore be indented.

IDE

At any point during the app building process, you can see your progress live on your mobile device or on the emulator. You'll want to use this feature while building your app, so you can see updates as soon as you make changes in the Designer to track your progress, and see how your app looks on your device. Since we've made some changes, let's connect now, so you can get familiar with the process. As you've already done the technical setup in *Chapter 2*, *Setting Up MIT App Inventor 2*, you can easily start using the Integrated Development Environment (IDE).

For users with mobile devices: on your computer in the Designer window, go to the top menu bar, click on Connect, and from the drop-down menu, select **AI Companion**, as shown in the following screenshot:

A pop-up window will appear on your computer screen with a QR code and a six-character code. Launch the AI2 Companion app on your mobile device and either scan the QR code or type in the six-character code. Note that to scan the QR code, you need to press the blue button on your mobile device that says **scan QR code** and then hold the mobile device up to the computer screen to capture the image. Scanning the QR code with your mobile device will automatically launch your Fling app after a few moments. To connect with the code, type the six-character code shown on your computer screen into the white text box on your mobile device and then click on the orange button **Connect with code** to display the Fling app on your mobile device.

For users without mobile devices: On your computer in the Designer window, go to the top menu bar, click on **Connect** and, from the drop-down menu, select **Emulator**, as shown in the following screenshot:

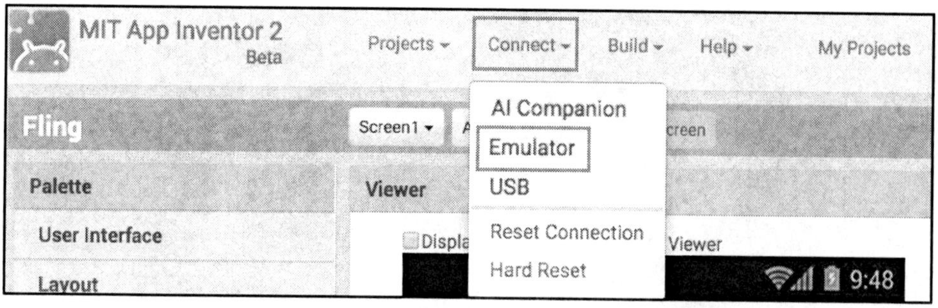

The emulator will take a few minutes to launch. You will see pop-up messages about the progress and the status of the emulator (to review connecting with the emulator, please see *Chapter 2, Setting Up MIT App Inventor 2*).

Note that at any point throughout the app building process, if you have trouble connecting or if the modes of connection are grayed out, you may need to choose **Reset Connection** from the drop-down menu, as shown in the next screenshot:

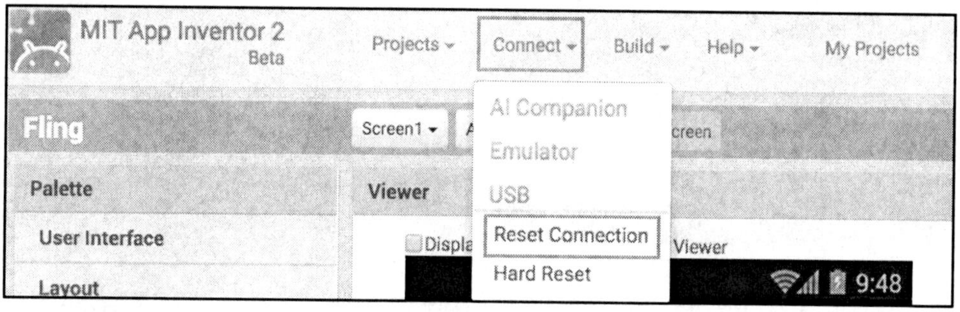

After clicking on Reset Connection, the choices for connecting will become clickable again. Choose the method you previously used: **AI Companion** or **Emulator** (remember, for WiFi connection to work, your computer and mobile device must be on the same WiFi network). For connecting via USB, please review the instructions in *Chapter 2, Setting Up MIT App Inventor 2*.

Wait a few seconds after connecting and you will see one of the following images (the screenshot of a mobile device on the left-hand side and an emulator on the right-hand side):

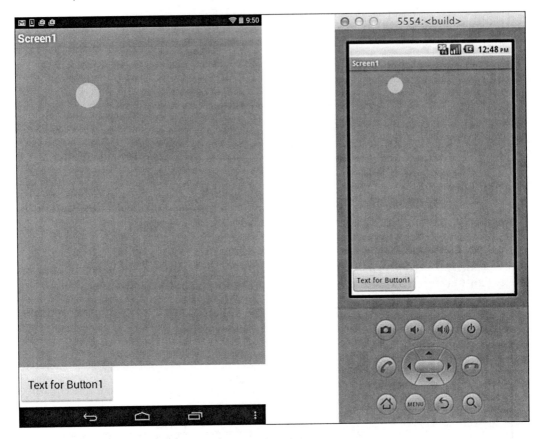

Now that you've connected your project to your mobile device or emulator, all the changes you make on your computer will automatically be updated on your device or emulator. This is particularly helpful because a component on your computer screen could be displayed somewhat differently on your mobile device or emulator. It is always a good idea to check periodically to see how your app is taking shape on your mobile device or emulator.

Let's go back to the Designer. You can change the look and the text of **Button1** by editing the **Properties**. Change the options to reflect the following screenshot:

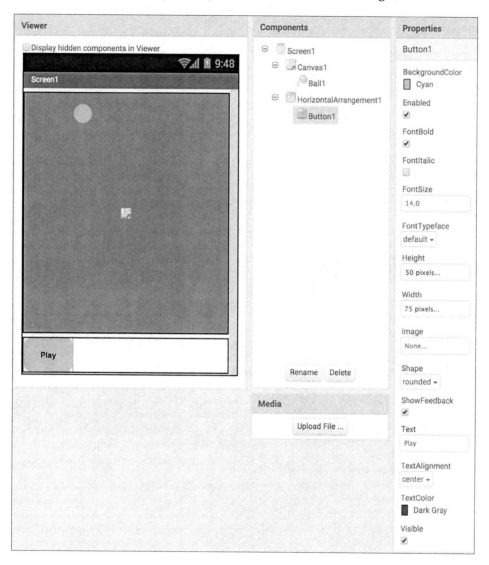

Notice how your mobile device or emulator also updates in real time and displays the changes you just made to Button1, as shown in the following images (the screenshot of a mobile device on the left-hand side and an emulator on the right-hand side):

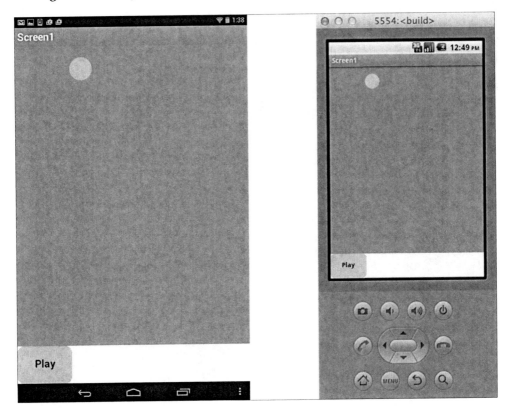

You are now going to add another **Button** to the **HorizontalArrangement** component.

When you drag the Button from the **User Interface** palette drawer, App Inventor will name this button as **Button2**, as shown in the next screenshot:

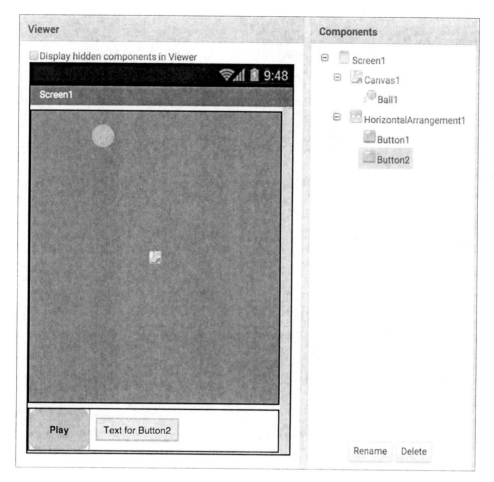

Notice how your mobile device or emulator also updates in real time, as shown in the next images (the screenshot of a mobile device on the left-hand side and an emulator on the right-hand side):

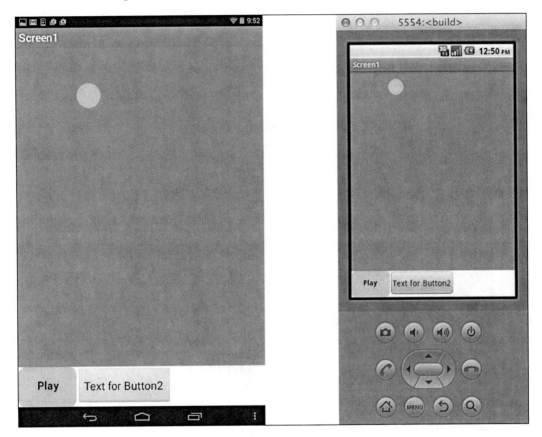

It is always a good practice to rename your components when you have more than one of a kind, or to reflect what they will do. Soon your apps will have multiple buttons, screens, and more. So, it's helpful to use specific names. **Button1** is the **Play** button, so let's rename it accordingly. Click on **Button1**, so it is highlighted in the **Components** panel. Then, click on **Rename** at the bottom of the panel. A pop-up window will give you the option to type in a new name, as shown in the next screenshot:

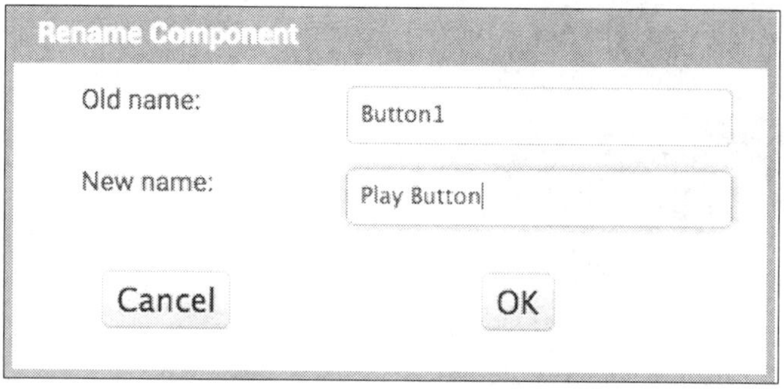

Rename Component

Old name:

Button1

New name:

Play Button

Cancel   OK

You will see the new name listed in the Components panel. Note that App Inventor converted the space between the two words into an underscore.

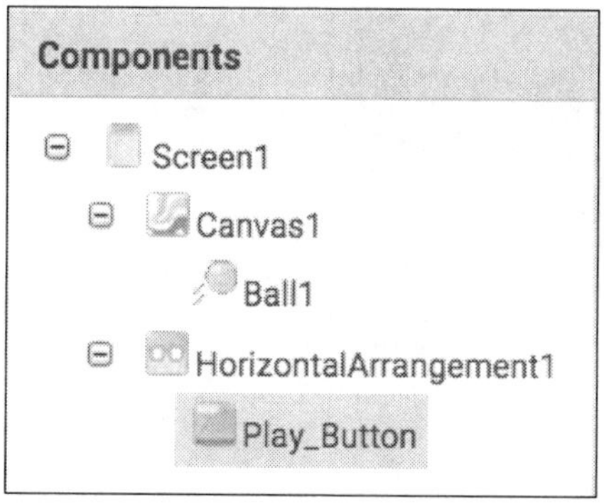

Components

⊖ ☐ Screen1
  ⊖ Canvas1
      Ball1
  ⊖ HorizontalArrangement1
      Play_Button

Note that if we had changed the name of Button1 to Play_Button before adding the second button, when you dragged out the second button, it would've been named as Button1. This can be confusing, so it's always a good idea to rename your components rather than keeping track of the order you added them, especially because in this case, Button1 would not have been the first button you added, but the second one.

Repeat the steps listed earlier to rename **Button2** to **Reset** button. Then, edit the **Properties** of **Reset_Button** as shown in the following screenshot:

 Note that while we changed the names of the **Button** components to **Play_Button** and **Reset_Button**, the text on the buttons remains what we typed in the text fields: **Play** and **Reset**, respectively.

Viewer	Components	Properties

Viewer

☐ Display hidden components in Viewer

📶📶 🔋 9:48

Screen1

Play Reset

Components

⊟ ☐ Screen1
  ⊟ 🖼 Canvas1
    🔍 Ball1
  ⊟ 🖼 HorizontalArrangement1
    ☐ Play_Button
    ☐ Reset_Button

Rename Delete

Media

Upload File ...

Properties

Replay_Button

BackgroundColor
☐ Cyan

Enabled
☑

FontBold
☑

FontItalic
☐

FontSize
14.0

FontTypeface
default ▾

Height
50 pixels...

Width
75 pixels...

Image
None...

Shape
rounded ▾

ShowFeedback
☑

Text
Replay

TextAlignment
center ▾

TextColor
⬛ Dark Gray

Visible
☑

Notice how your mobile device or emulator also updates in real time. Here is a good example of why you would want to take advantage of the Integrated Development Environment. As you can see in the previous screenshot, a space appears between the two buttons in the designer, but on the mobile device (in this case, a tablet) and on the emulator, there is no space, as shown in the following screenshot. By continuously monitoring how your app looks (and later functions) on your device as you build it, you are ensuring at each step of the way that your app will appear and work as you intended.

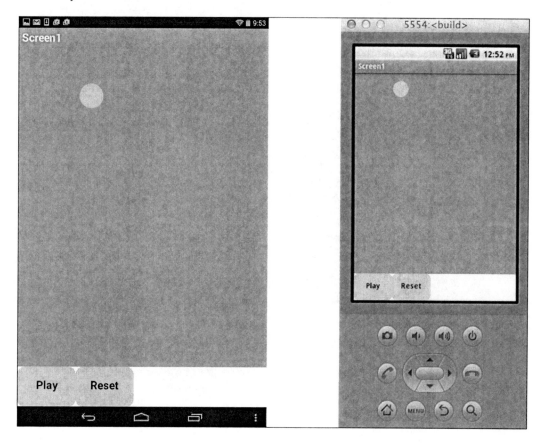

Now, we are going to add a Label to display some text (and ultimately the score). Go to the Palette **User Interface** drawer and drag out a **Label** onto **HorizontalArrangement**. You can place it anywhere you want in the menu bar, but for the purpose of this tutorial, we will drag it in between the **Play** and **Replay** buttons. Adjust the label properties to reflect this in the next screenshot and rename the Label Component to **Score** (note that underneath the **Text** property, we have deleted **Text for Label1**, so it appears empty).

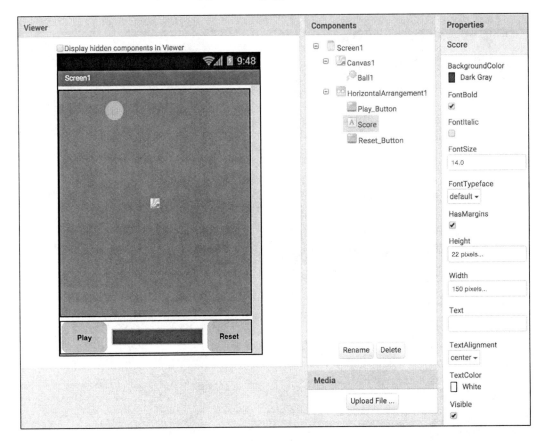

Congratulations! You have completed designing the UI of the Fling app! Notice how nothing happens to the ball when either of the buttons is pushed. This is because we haven't programmed the behavior of the Components yet. Next, we will switch to the Blocks Editor to start coding.

The Blocks editor

To switch to the Blocks editor, click on the **Blocks** button in the upper-right corner of the menu bar.

The Blocks window has a Blocks panel (left), a Viewer (the large white workspace), and a Media panel (in the lower-left corner). The Media panel operates in the same manner as the designer, although we won't be using it for this app.

All the tools you need to program your app are in the Blocks panel on the left-hand side of the window. The first set of Blocks shown with small colored boxes is called Built-in (you will learn about these as we build our app). Below the Built-in blocks are the blocks relating to the Components you just added in the Designer. Below the Component blocks is a list of Any Component blocks. We will not be using these in this chapter.

Navigating the Blocks editor is similar to the Designer. When you click on a block in the Blocks panel, a pop-up drawer will appear to reveal many colored puzzle-like blocks. The block you click on will automatically appear in the white workspace called the Viewer. To program your app, you need to drag one block into another, and hear and see it snap into place.

Once you start filling up the Viewer with blocks, it can get crowded. There are two ways to use more of the workspace: by using the bottom and side gray scroll bars or by clicking and dragging on the white space itself. This will become evident once the blocks are in place.

The Blocks drawer

When you click on any of the blocks' categories in the Blocks panel, a pop-up drawer of available blocks will appear. The following screenshot shows some of the available blocks for the Play_Button component (the gray scroll bar indicates that there are more blocks than what is shown on the screen. You can see the rest of the blocks by scrolling down):

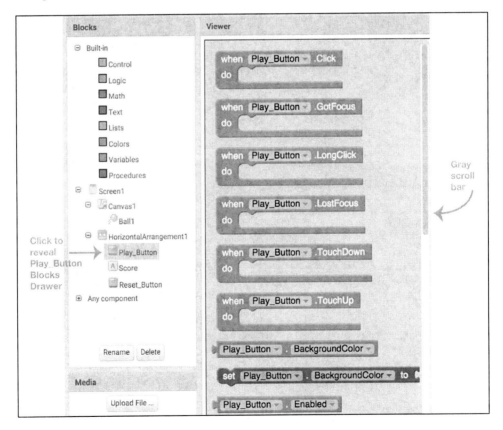

Types of Blocks

Component Blocks are made up of different kinds of blocks. For this app, we will be using three kinds of blocks: **event**, **setters**, and **getters**.

- **Event Blocks**: They are gold, and if they exist for a certain component, they will appear at the top of any pop-up Blocks drawer. They launch an event, such as **when Play_Button.Click**. To program what happens when the **Play** button is clicked, you can snap together other puzzle piece blocks called setters and getters.

- **Setters**: They are dark green or orange puzzle piece blocks that say set because they set a property's value. Notice that setters have an opening at the end. Another type of block, a getter, fits into that space and so the setter can get a value.

- **Getters**: They are colored puzzle piece blocks that fit at the end of the setters. They give a property value to the setters.

Built-in blocks have a variety of different colors and purposes. We will explain them as we use them.

Using Blocks to program Fling

We will now begin using blocks to code our app.

The Play button

Click on **Play_Button** in the **Blocks** panel to open its drawer. Then, click on the top gold **when Play_Button.Click** event block as shown in the next screenshot. It will now appear in the **Viewer**.

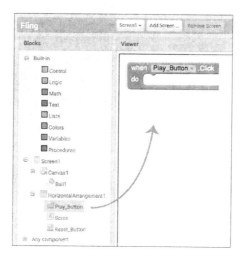

When a user clicks on the app's **Play** button, we want the game to begin and the ball to start moving. So, we need to program these steps.

First of all, we are going to position the ball at the top of the screen and have it move down toward the bottom of the screen. But we don't want to set it all the way at the top of the screen because, in the next chapter, we are going to program our app, so that, every time the ball hits the top edge, the user will score a point. To avoid scoring points by merely pressing Play or Reset, we must position the ball a little below the top edge. To do this, we need to set a pair of the (x, y) values for the Canvas. The x value is where the ball will be horizontally on the screen and the y value will be the ball's vertical position. The x value is defined as the number of pixels from the left edge of the Canvas and y is defined as the number of pixels from the top edge of the Canvas. We decided that we don't want y to be 0, as the ball would be touching the edge, so we can set the y value to something close to 0, such as 2. We can set the x value to any value along the width of the Canvas. To make the game more unpredictable, we will program the app to pick a random value for x. Then, each time the user hits Play or Reset, the ball will start at a different location horizontally on the screen (although it will always start 2 pixels from the top, since we are setting y = 2). To set the ball's starting location, we will select a block from the Ball1 drawer.

Click on **Ball1** in the **Blocks** panel. A drawer will open with all the available blocks for **Ball1**. Use the gray scroll bar to the right of the pop-up drawer to scroll down past the gold event blocks. Click on the purple procedure block: **call Ball1.MoveTo x, y**, as shown in the next screenshot:

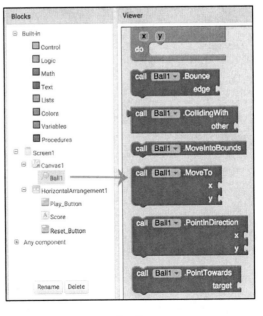

The purple procedure block will now appear next to the **when Play_Button.Click** gold event block in the **Viewer**. Notice how the shape of this purple block fits inside the gold block. Go ahead and place it into the gold block (by clicking on it with your mouse and dragging it). The gold block will expand to accommodate the purple block. You will hear and see it snap into place, as shown in the following screenshot on the right-hand side:

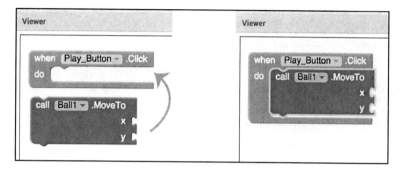

We know that we want the value of **y** to be equal to 2, so we will find a block (a getter) to get this value. Click on the **Math** block in the **Built-in** section. The **Built-in Math** blocks have a little blue box next to it. A drawer will open up with the available blue **Math** getter blocks. Click on the first one with the value of **0**, as shown in the next screenshot:

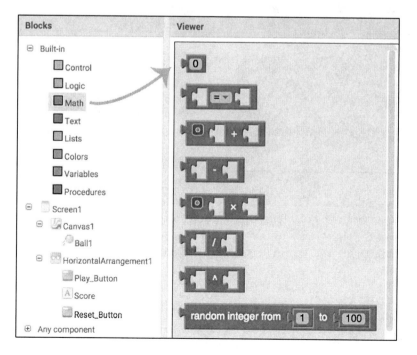

The **0** block will appear in the **Viewer**, and you can drag it and snap it to the *y* value. Click on **0** to highlight it. You can type in the number 2 to change the value to 2, as shown in the following screenshot. Next, we are going to set the *x* value to a random integer. Go back to the **Math** blocks and click on the last block shown in the preceding screenshot: **random integer from 1 to 100**. Drag this block to the *x* value, as shown next:

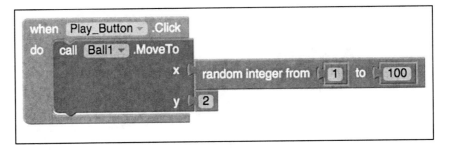

Since users will have mobile devices with different screen sizes, we won't know whether the width will be 100 pixels or 350 pixels. So, to enable the game to be played on different size screens, we can remove the **Math** block with the value of **100** and insert a getter block instead that will get the screen width of the mobile device the user is using. To delete the blue **100** block, click on it to outline it in yellow. A little hand icon will appear. This indicates that you can drag the block out of the slot, as shown in the following screenshot:

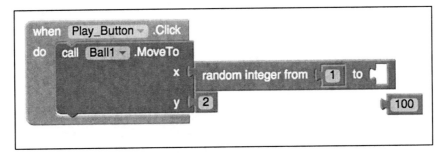

Note that if you don't see the hand icon, it just means that you clicked on the actual number instead of the block. This will be indicated by a cursor and a little bit of white space to the right of the number. Click again on the actual blue part of the number puzzle piece and you will see the hand icon, which will allow you to drag the block out.

To delete this block (or any unwanted block), click on it (if it is not already highlighted in yellow) and hit *Delete* on your computer's keyboard. Or, you can drag the block to the lower-right corner of the Viewer to throw it in the trash. Hover the block over the trash can and the lid will open. When you release the block, it will disappear. You will see it fade away and hear a crumple sound.

To add the a block indicating the user's screen width block, click on **Screen1** in the **Blocks** palette and choose **Screen1.Width** from the drawer. It will be near the bottom, so you can use the gray scroll bar to scroll down and find it.

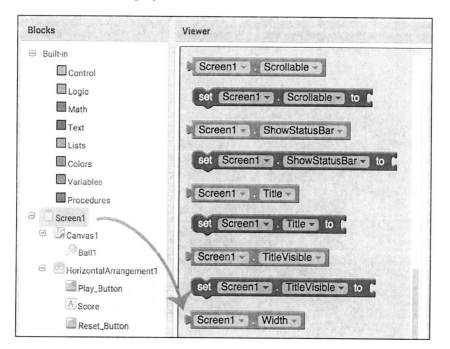

Note that to drop this block inside another block (whether an equation or a single block), align the little puzzle piece nib on the left-hand side of the block with the nib space on the left-hand side of the block's opening and it will easily snap into place. Your blocks should look as follows:

Every time a user presses **Play**, the ball will be positioned at a different place along the width of the screen and **2** pixels from the top of the screen.

Now that we have positioned the ball, we will now program it to move.

Moving the ball

Since we've programmed the ball to start at the top of the screen, we want the ball to move downward. Instead of it just dropping straight down or at the same angle each time, we can set the degrees to be random. There are 360 degrees in a circle, but we only want the ball to fall between certain degrees, those represented as downward that fit between the width of the screen, but not along the edges of the screen. The figure below shows that the right edge is **0** degrees and the left edge is **180** degrees. The actual space that we are interested in is the lower half or the degrees between **180** and **360**. Since we don't want the ball to just travel down the edges, we will eliminate the two extremes when choosing some numbers. We decided to choose degrees between **200** and **340**. We will code the app so that the program will choose a random number between those degrees for the angle at which the ball will move.

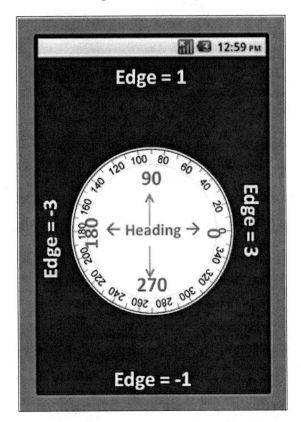

You already learned how to program a random integer from our previous blocks, so let's repeat those steps. Go to the **Math** blocks and choose the blue **random integer from to** block. You also know how to fill in these numbers. To review, choose the topmost blue block in the **Math** blocks: the one with **0**. You can enter **200** in it and then copy and paste the block by clicking on it to highlight it (make sure it has a yellow outline). If you don't want to copy and paste, you can always drag out another **Math 0** block. Click on the number in the copied block and type **340**. Then, place the **200** block into the **from** spot and the 340 block into the **to** spot.

Our **random integer from to** block needs to fit someplace, to which block will it be giving this information? Another way to ask this question is: which block will be getting this information? If you guessed Ball, you are correct! The ball will need this information to know the angle at which it has to move. So, we need to find the ball block that represents the ball's direction. This block is called **Ball1.Heading**, and it represents the degrees the ball will move. Click on the **Ball1** Blocks drawer to find the dark green **Ball1.Heading** block (you will need to scroll down past the gold and purple blocks to find it). Once this is on your **Viewer**, snap it together with the blue **random integer from to** block that you just created. Then, take these connected pieces and insert them at the bottom of the gold **when Play_Button.Click**. Your blocks should now look like the following screenshot:

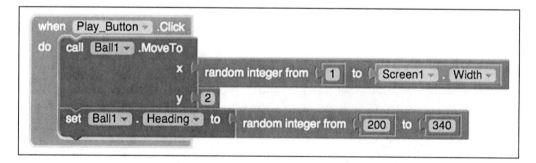

Now that we have the location of the ball and the direction it is heading in degrees, we need to program it to actually move. To do this, we will first set the ball to enabled. From the **Ball1** blocks drawer, choose the dark green **set Ball1.Enabled to** block. Then, from the **Logic** blocks drawer, choose the lime green **true** block at the top, as shown in the next screenshot:

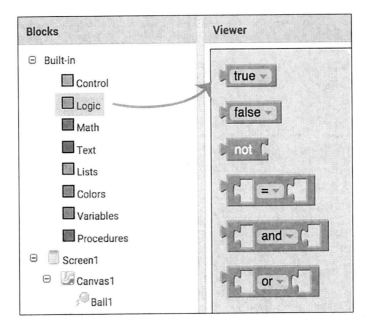

Insert the **true** block into the **set Ball1.Enabled to** block and add them to the bottom of the **when Play_Button.Click** event, as shown in the following screenshot:

Now that the ball is ready to move, we can actually move it by setting the speed and the interval. Go back to the **Ball1** Blocks drawer and select the dark green setter block, **set Ball1.Speed**. Next, from the same drawer, select **set Ball1.Interval**.

The interval is the amount of time, in milliseconds (*1000 milliseconds = 1 second*), the ball will travel, and the speed is the number of pixels the ball will move in that timeframe. It's fun to play around with these numbers to see how fast or slow you can make the ball move. We've decided to have the ball move **10** pixels every **50** milliseconds, so we will program our blocks to look as follows:

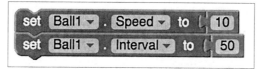

Insert these blocks at the bottom of the **when Play_Button.Click** event. Your blocks will look like the following screenshot:

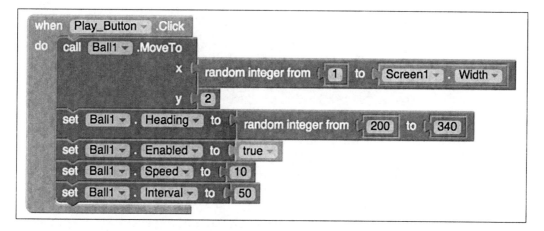

So far, this is what our app does: when the **Play** button is clicked, it will move the ball to position it **2** pixels away from the top edge of the screen and to a random number between **1** pixel from the left edge of the screen and the right edge of the screen. It will set the ball rolling downward in a random direction (between the degrees **200** to **340**) at a speed of **10** pixels every **50** milliseconds!

Flinging the ball

The object of the game is to fling the downward moving ball away from the bottom edge, because if the ball drops down to the bottom edge of the screen, the game will end. Next, we need to code these events.

First, let's program the app to fling the ball.

How will the ball know when a finger touches it and how to move in another direction (not downward)? We can program these events by using a block from the **Ball1** Blocks drawer called **when Ball1.Flung**. Click on this gold event block to add it to the Viewer. You can make the ball move at any speed you like, but we are going to keep it going at the same speed, just in a different direction. To do this, you can copy and paste the **set Ball1.Speed to** and **set Ball1.Interval to** blocks from the **when Play_Button.Click** event (note that when you click on the dark green set block and copy and paste it, the blue getter block attached to it will also copy and paste). Add these blocks to the **when Ball1.Flung** event to resemble the following screenshot:

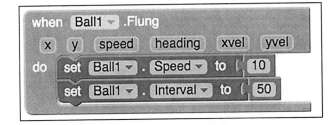

Next, we will reposition the direction of the ball to go upward (when it is flung by a finger). We could set the heading to a degree between 10 and 170 (see *image #39*) or we could make the ball go in the upward direction with an equation. Let's practice equations more. Copy and paste the **set Ball1.Heading** block from the **when Play_Button.Click** event (remember the heading block determines the angle at which the ball will move). Drag it to the bottom of the **when Ball1.Flung** event. We want the ball to go in the opposite direction than the direction in which it was heading, not to a random integer, so you can delete the attached blue block by highlighting it and pressing **delete** on your keyboard or by clicking on the blue block and dragging it to trash. To get the ball to go in the opposite direction, we are going to subtract the current ball's heading (direction) from 360 degrees (the total number of degrees possible). To code this, choose the minus block from the **Math Blocks** drawer. In the first open space, add the number **360**. Copy and paste the **50** blue block from the **when Ball1.Flung** event and change the number to **360**. Insert it into the open space to the left of the minus sign.

Next, from the **Ball1** Blocks drawer, select the light green getter block, **Ball1. Heading**. Insert it in the open space to the right of the minus sign (line up the block nib with the open nib). Here is what we have coded: when the ball is touched and flung, the program will move the ball's direction (or heading) to 360 degrees minus the old direction (or heading). Your blocks will look like the next screenshot:

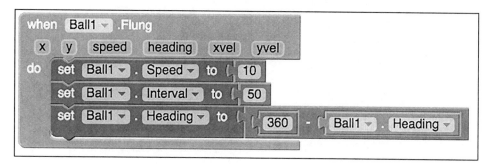

Ending the game or bouncing the ball

Now that the Play Button starts the ball moving downward and the user can fling it in a different direction, we want to program the following actions:

- Ending the game when the ball touches the bottom edge
- Bouncing the ball off the left, top, and right edges

We can program these actions with the **if/then** blocks. If the ball touches the bottom edge, **then** the ball will stop and the game will end. **If** the ball touches the other edges, **then** the ball will bounce back and the game will continue.

Let's first program the app to stop and end the game when the ball hits the bottom edge. App Inventor makes this easy. Go to the **Ball1** Blocks drawer and click on the **when Ball1.EdgeReached** event. Once the event block is in the Viewer, hover (don't click) on the light orange word **edge** on the left-hand side of the block and you will get a popup, as shown in the next screenshot. Choose the top dark orange **get edge** block. This is a variable. Set it aside; we will use it in a minute.

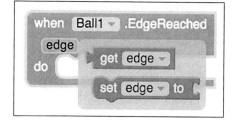

We will add an **if then** event to the inside of the when **Ball1.EdgeReached** event. But first we will configure it. Go to the topmost **Blocks** drawer called **Control** and click on the first gold **if then** block.

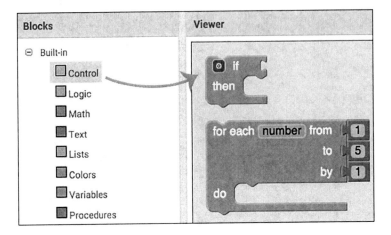

When the block first appears on your **Viewer**, it will look like *Step 1* in the following image. If you click on the blue color square in the upper-left corner, a popup will appear. Move your cursor over the bottom **else** block on the left-hand side of the popup, click on it, and drag it into the **if** opening on the right-hand side of the popup, as shown in *Step 2* and *Step 3*. Once the **else** block is in place, you will see the original **if then** event block change into an **if then else** block. You will see that **else** is now added to the bottom of the block, as shown in *Step 3* and *Step 4*:

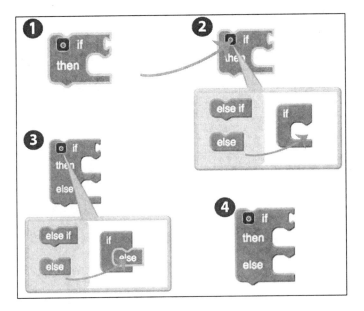

Add this **if then else** block to the inside of the when **Ball1.EdgeReached** block, as shown in the following screenshot:

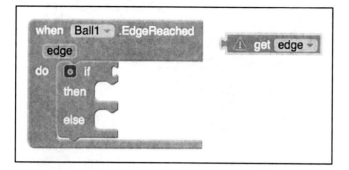

> Notice how the get edge block that we set aside has an exclamation point with a triangle around it. This is an error message alerting you that the block is unattached and is in need of a setter block.

To program, **if** the ball touches the bottom edge, **then** the ball will stop and the game will end. We will use a **math equals** block. It is the second one from the top in the **Math Blocks** drawer, as shown in the next screenshot:

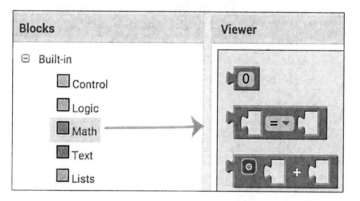

Inside the first opening to the left of the equal sign, add the dark orange **get edge** block that we had set aside. You will notice that the alert will remain on this block until we snap the math block in place with the **if** block, which we will do shortly.

In the next image, you will see that each edge is represented by a number:

Since the bottom edge is equal to **-1**, add a number Math block to this equal block and enter the number **-1**. Snap the blue math block into the **if** block, as shown below (and you will see the alert disappear).

When the bottom edge is reached, we want the ball to stop, the game to end, and the app to display the text **Game Over**. We already know how to enable the ball to move: we set the property enabled to **true**. So, now that we want the ball to stop or not move, we must set the enabled property to **false**. In the **Ball1** blocks drawer, select **set Ball1.Enabled to** and then in the **Logic** blocks drawer select the **false** block. Slide that set of blocks into the **then** space of the **if then else** block, as shown below.

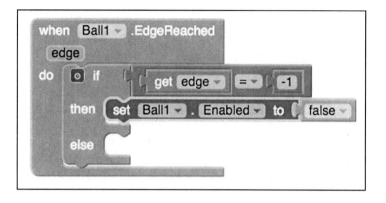

Next, we will program the app to display some text indicating that the game is over. We will use the Label that we named **Score** (in the next chapter, we will also use this Label to display the score). Go to the **Score** blocks drawer and select the dark green **set Score.Text to** block, as shown in the following screenshot:

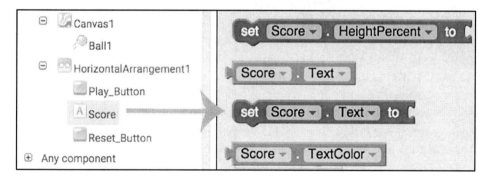

This setter block needs to get some text, so we will add a getter text block. Go to the pink **Text** block drawer and choose the first block, which is an empty space with quotes around it, as shown in the next screenshot:

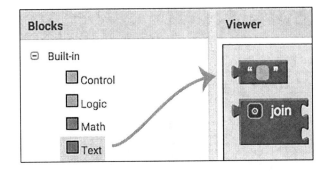

You will add this pink text block to the **set Score.Text to** block and insert it below the **set Ball1.Enabled to** block in the **then** event. Click on the pink text block and type the words **Game Over**, as follows:

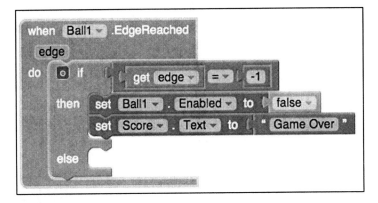

We have programmed the app so that if the ball hits the bottom edge, it will stop moving and the Label will display the text: **Game Over**.

The last step, the **else** block, is for when the ball hits an edge other than **-1** (the bottom). If the ball hits any of the other edges, we want the ball to bounce off them and the gameplay to continue. To program this, we'll use the purple **call Ball1.Bounce** block. We will attach the same orange **get edge** block we used previously, but this time, we won't specify a certain edge. Any edge that the ball touches, other than the bottom edge, will cause the ball to bounce. Copy and paste the **get edge block**, add it to the purple **call Ball1.Bounce** block, and insert the blocks into the **else** slot, as follows:

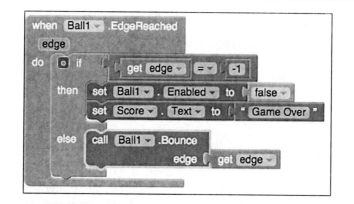

Think of **else** as meaning *otherwise*. If the ball hits an edge equal to **-1**, then execute the **then** code, otherwise execute the **else** code. In other words, if the **if** option is not met (if the ball doesn't hit the **-1** edge), then the program will skip **then** and jump to **else**.

Following is a screenshot of our app when the ball hits the bottom edge, stops, and displays **Game Over**.

The Reset button

The last thing we will do in this chapter is configure the **Reset** button. The **Reset** button gets pressed after the game has ended due to the ball hitting the bottom edge. It doesn't start the gameplay like the **Play** button does; it merely repositions the ball back at the top of the screen and makes the **Game Over** text disappear from the screen (Label).

Go into the **Reset Button** Blocks and choose the gold event **when Reset_Button. Click**. We want to move the ball from the bottom of the screen to the top of the screen. We already know how to do this because we did it for the Play Button. You can copy and paste the call **Ball1.MoveTo** purple block (when you click on the purple block and copy and paste it, it will automatically copy and paste the blue *x, y*, getter blocks attached to it). Add your blocks to the **when Reset_Button.Click** event, and your blocks will look like the following screenshot:

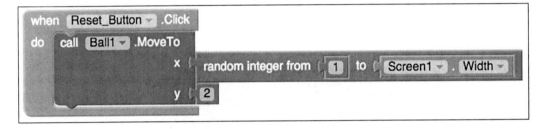

These blocks reposition the ball back up to the top of the screen (to a random **x** location), but the **Game Over** text will still be displayed. To have the Reset Button erase this, we will simply set the **Score Text** to blank text instead of **Game Over**. Copy and paste the dark green **set Score.Text to** block from the **when Ball1. EdgeReached** event block (copying and pasting the green Setter block will also copy and paste the pink text block). Click on the **Game Over** text and press *Delete*, so the text area is empty. Add this set of blocks to the bottom of the **when Reset_Button. Click** event block, as follows:

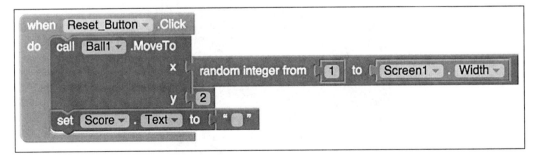

The following is a screenshot of our app after the **Reset** button is pressed. It shows the ball up at the top of the screen and a blank area where the **Game Over** text previously appeared.

Our first version of the Fling app is now complete! We have designed and coded the Fling app, so when the Play Button is clicked, it will randomly position the ball at the top of the screen and start the ball rolling downward. Flinging the ball with a finger causes the ball to move in the opposite direction to than was going. The ball bounces of all the edges, except for the bottom one. When the ball hits the bottom edge, it stops and the app displays **Game Over**. The **Reset** button repositions the ball to a random position at the top of the screen. At this point, you may or may not have discovered that we have a bug! It has something to do with the Play and Reset buttons. We will reveal and fix this bug in the next chapter.

Summary

Wow! You have learned a great deal about the App Inventor platform in this chapter and you have built and programmed your first app! This is a huge accomplishment! But, as you may have noticed, we have an issue to fix. We will demonstrate not only how to debug your first bug, but also how to add more features. Really, this is just the beginning of your mobile computing adventure. There is much more to learn and create! Our Fling app is functional and simple, but I'm sure you can think of countless more features to enhance it. In the next chapter, you will learn how to expand the app's complexity by creating a scoring mechanism that is displayed when the ball touches the top edge, by allowing the ball to be flung only from the lower half of the screen, and by creating levels and increasing the speed of the ball

By learning how to add more functionality to an existing app, you will gain experience developing multiple versions. This process of building an app with added features is what developers regularly do. Ultimately, once you post your app in an app market like Google Play, the new versions would be released as updates.

Let's take our game to the next level!

4
Fling App – Part 2

In *Chapter 3, Navigating the App Inventor Platform*, you learned to use the MIT App Inventor Designer and Blocks Editor by creating your first fully functional mobile app! In this chapter, we will show you how you can take the basic Fling app and build it out by adding more complex features. We will demonstrate how to enable:

- A scoring mechanism that will display when the ball touches the top edge
- Code, so the ball can only be flung from the lower half of the screen
- The increasing levels of difficulty by increasing ball speed

We will also begin debugging. Debugging is a standard practice in app development and should be viewed as part of the process, not as something negative.

Each time you add new components to your app, we encourage you to share your app with others to get feedback. Not only will the feedback give you ideas about the design, but it will also help you learn what users want from an app game. Such information will prove invaluable once you begin designing apps from scratch. This chapter will not only help you discover new ways to enhance a game app, it will also trigger new paths of creativity! By the end of this chapter, your Fling app will resemble the following image:

Adding a scoring feature

Since most game apps include some sort of scoring feature, we will add this code to our Fling app. The score will display in the same label that will also display the **Game Over** text.

Coding scoring blocks

We left off in the last chapter with the ball bouncing off all the edges except the bottom edge. Now, we want to program the app to increase the score by one point every time the ball reaches the top edge. We will use another **if/then** block and add it into the **else** portion of the existing **if/then/else** block within the **when Ball1. EdgeReached** event, as shown in the following screenshot:

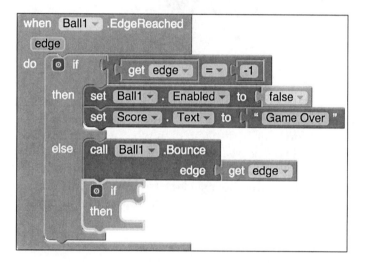

Can you guess what block will fit in the **if** opening? If the ball hits the top edge, then the app will increase the score by **1**. In *Chapter 3, Navigating the App Inventor Platform*, you learned that the bottom edge is represented by **-1** (and the top edge is represented by 1). Since we've already created an if/then scenario for the ball hitting the bottom edge, we can copy this set of blocks and adjust it for the ball hitting the top edge.

Copy the blue block from the existing **if** block (note that by copying the blue block, you will also automatically copy the embedded orange **get edge** block and the blue **-1** math block). Snap these pasted blocks into the new **if** block and change **-1** to **1**, as shown in the following screenshot:

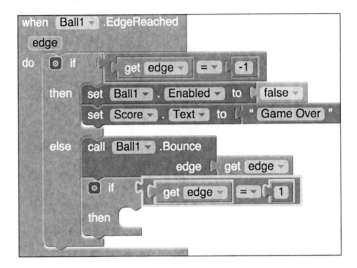

We have coded: if the top edge is reached, then what will happen? We want the app to record a point. To code the score feature, we will first create a **global variable**. A global variable is a value that can be used by any block, whereas a **local variable** is one that can only be used by the specific block for which it was intended. Go to the **Variables** block drawer and select the orange, **initialize global name to** block.

Click on **name** and change the text to **score**. Next, in the **Math** drawer, select the **0** blue Math block. Connect it to the **initialize global score to** block. Your blocks will now look like the following screenshot. Note that this **initialize global name** block does not fit into any other block; it stands alone with the attached Math **0** block.

initialize global score to 0

By setting the global variable equal to **0**, essentially, we have established the initial score to be set to 0. Now, we can program the app to add **1** to this score. Go back into the **Variables** block drawer and select the **set to** block. Click on the little arrow in the middle of the block and select **global score** from the drop-down menu (this is now available for us to select because we created the global variable). Insert the block into the empty **then** slot, as shown in the following screenshot:

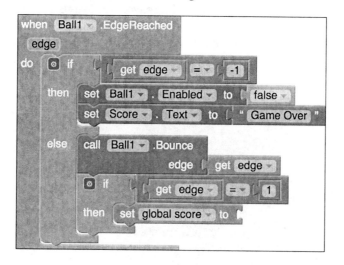

You will insert a Math block into the **set global score to** block because, every time the top edge is reached, we will want to get the current score (in this case, **0**) and add **1** to it. Therefore, we will need the blue Math addition block, as shown in the following screenshot:

The first blank will be filled with an orange **get global score** block, in the second block after the plus sign, there will be a number block filled with **1**, as shown in the following screenshot. There are two ways to find the get global score block. One is in the Variables drawer. Click on the get to block and then click on the downward arrow to select global score from the drop down menu. Or, you can hover (not click) over the initialize global score block and both a set and get global score block will appear. Select the get global score block. The reason we are using the get global score block and not the 0 block is because we want to add 1 to the most recent score. At the beginning of the game, the score is 0, but as soon as the ball hits the top edge, the new global score will be 0+1, then 1+1 (and so on):

So now, we have created the code to update the score each time the top edge is reached. But we haven't yet created the code to display the score. Let's do this next.

Updating the score label

Take a look at the blocks in the first **then** section in the following screenshot and notice the name change of our Score Label. Since the Score Label will be displaying both the score and the level, we decided to make that clear in our label name. In the Designer, we renamed the Label from Score to Score_Level_Label. This change updates in the Blocks Editor as well. The block name initially was, set Score.Text to is now, set Score_Level_Label.Text to. The blocks drawer is also updated. We show you this edit in the middle of development because sometimes, no matter how well thought out your app is, you may discover ways to improve it as you begin coding. Changing the Label name is not necessarily integral to the functioning of our app, but it helps us to be more clear in our design

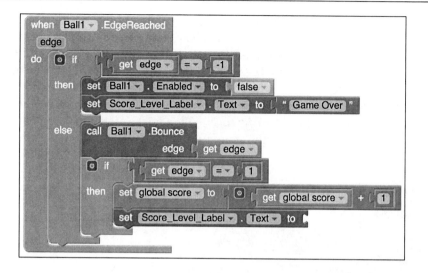

Since the Label will now display both the score and the level, we need to code that. Copy the green **set Score_Level_Label.Text to** block, from the if/then/else block. Since it will also copy the pink **"Game Over"** text block, you can merely delete this block as we won't need it. Instead, go into the pink **Text** blocks and choose the **join** block, as shown in the following screenshot:

We need this block to set the Label text to display pieces of information: the score and the level. If you think about it, we can't just display two numbers because the user won't know what they mean. We have to display: the word **Score** and the actual score (whatever number it is) and the word "Level" and the actual level (whatever number that is). To begin, we will just add two things, the word Score and the actual score. You probably can guess that the first block to attach to the join block is another blank **Text** block will. Type the word **Score:** with a space after the colon (so there will be a space between the word and the score number). The second block is the orange **get global score** block.

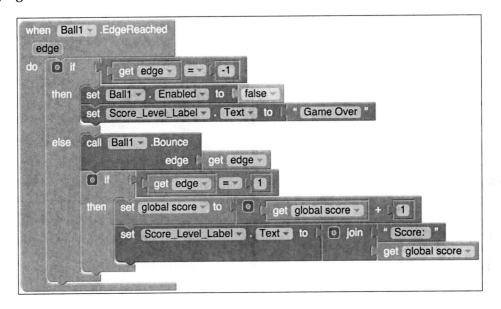

Increasing difficulty

If you stop and think about our app as it stands, it would be very easy to cheat! A user could just keep the ball very near the top edge and fling it a short distance to amass tons of points! If you'd like to make it harder for the user to score points, we will show you one way to increase the difficulty. If, on the other hand, you are making this app for a young user and want it to be easy for them to score points, then you can skip this section.

Changing the game's dynamic

As the game stands, the ball is moving downward and whenever your finger touches it, it will get flung in another direction (to be exact, 360 degrees minus the direction it was heading). We can program the app so the ball only responds to a fling when it is below the middle of the screen. Can you guess how we might program this? If you guessed using an **if/then** block, you're on the right track! If the ball is below the middle of the screen, then it can be flung.

Currently, our blocks look like the following screenshot:

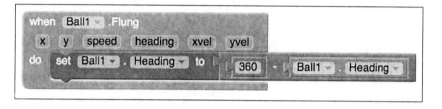

We want to tell the app to first check and see whether the ball is below the middle of the screen. We've coded something similar if you recall when we used the **Screen1. Width** block. Since we won't know the screen size of every user, we cannot just input a specific number and divide it by 2. But we can get the user's screen size with the **Screen1.Height** block and divide this by 2. In *Chapter 3, Navigating the App Inventor Platform*, you also learned that **x** is used to represent the width and **y** is used to represent the height. The values of **x** and **y** start with 0, 0 in the top left corner of the screen. So, we will use the **y** variable, which represents the height. We know that **y** gets bigger from top to bottom. Thus, we want to enable the ball to be flung if **y** is bigger than the screen size divided by 2. For example, suppose that the height of the screen is 100 (with the value of 0 at the top and the value of 100 at the bottom). If the ball is at *y* = *51*, it will be just below the halfway mark. Thus, it will be enabled to be flung.

To begin coding this scenario temporarily, remove **set Ball1.Heading** and its accompanying blocks from the when Ball1.Flung event block. Add an **if/then** block and a **greater than Math** block (select the equals Math block and then chose the greater than symbol from the drop down menu by clicking on the downward arrow in the center of the block) to the **if** opening, as shown in the following screenshot:

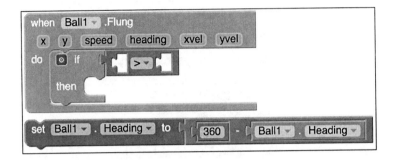

Next, hover over (don't click on) the light orange box with the variable y in the **when Ball1.Flung** event block. This will produce a pop-up window. Select the top choice, **get y**, as shown in the following screenshot:

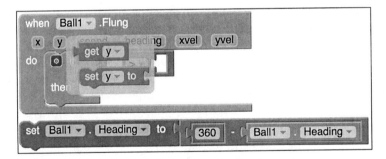

Insert the **get y** block into the first opening before the greater than sign. Remember we won't be adding a number into the second opening, but rather an equation of the screen height divided by 2.

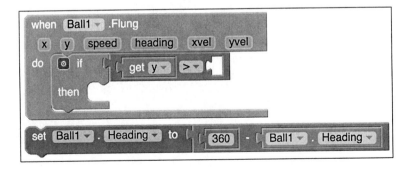

In the second opening, insert another **Math** block—this time, a division **Math** block because we want the **y** to be greater than the screen height divided by **2**. Get the **Screen1.Height** block from the **Screen1** block drawer and the **number** block from the **Math** drawer, and change the value to **2**. Insert the **Screen1.Height** block into the first opening of the **Math** division block and insert the number 2 block into the opening after the division sign.

Reinsert the set **Ball1.Heading** blocks you removed earlier into the **then** opening of the **if/then** block, as shown in the following screenshot:

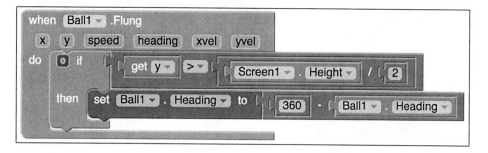

Now, our app checks to see *if* the ball's **y** height value is below the halfway point on the screen. If it is, *then* the ball will be flung in a direction indicated by our formula, **360 - Ball1.Heading**. If it is not, nothing will happen.

Creating levels

Computer games typically have multiple levels where the difficulty of playing the game progressively increases. This is what makes a game fun, challenging, and even somewhat addictive. We want to incorporate levels in our game as well.

One simple way to make the game play harder and harder is to increase the speed of the ball as the player continues to score points. You can create whatever tiers you like, but for the purpose of this tutorial, we will create a simple tier system: whenever a player scores 5 points, the player has completed a level. Again, to keep it simple, we will not pause game play (as is common in most computer games) when a level is completed. The player will automatically move on to the next level, which will also increase the speed of the ball.

To figure out whether a level change is needed or not, we will code the app to constantly check the value of score. Each time the score is incremented, the app will check to see whether it is a multiple of 5 (for example, *score = 5, 10, 15, 20, and so on*). If the score is indeed a multiple of 5, it will mean that the player has scored another 5 points and a level change should occur. To change the level, we will simply increase the speed a little bit.

As explained earlier in this chapter, the event, **Ball1.EdgeReached**, contains the code that increments the score: the **set global score to** block. Whenever the score increases, the label will update to display the new score (the previous score plus 1). As you can see in the blocks shown in the following screenshot, the block immediately after the score-increment block is the **set Score_Level_Label.text to** block to update the score displayed.

Now, we will add an **if/then** block right after the **set Score_Level_Label.text** block. Do you remember where to find the **if/then** block?

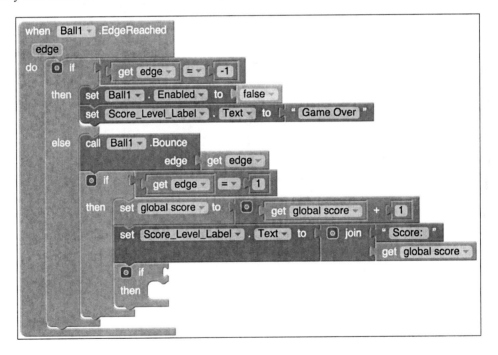

Now, let's think about the condition that we want to insert in the empty socket next to **if**. We want to check and see whether the score is a multiple of 5 (if it is a multiple of 5, then the remainder will be 0). In order to do so, we need to complete the following steps:

1. Get the current value of the score.

2. Divide its value by 5 and calculate the remainder.

3. See whether the remainder is equal to 0.

To achieve these three subtasks, we will first get the **get global score** block just like we did when we used this block to increment the score. This block can be select from the **Variables** blocks or can be copied from your current set of blocks. This completes task 1.

Next, we will get the remainder of the block from under the **Math** blocks. This step is not as obvious. When you go to the Math blocks, you will not see any remainder block. Instead, select the **modulo of** block, as shown in the following screenshot:

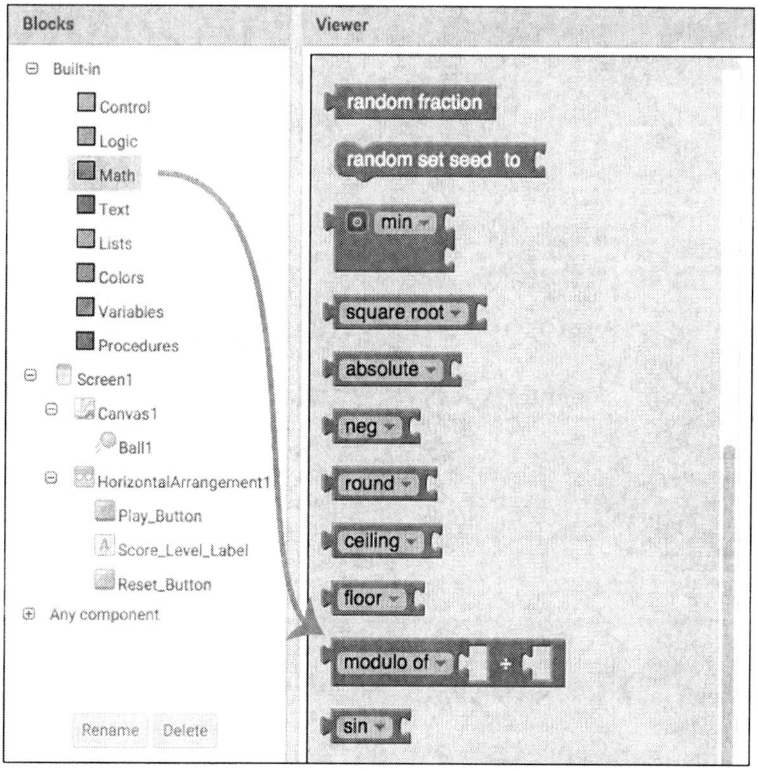

Click on the downward-facing triangle to the right of **modulo of** and select
remainder of from the drop-down list. Modulo, remainder, and quotient are
different mathematical operations related to division. Hence, they all belong to the
same block. Place the **get global score** block within the first slot of the **remainder of**
block. Since we want to calculate the remainder of the score when divided by 5, place
number **5** in the second slot of the **remainder of** block (that is, insert a Math number
block and change the value from 0 to 5). This completes step 2.

Finally, we want to check whether this remainder is equal to 0. If it is equal to 0, then
it is time to increase the level (speed). If it is not, the level (speed) will remain the
same. To check for the equality of numbers, we will need an **equal to** block from the
Math blocks. Plug the **remainder of** block (and its accompanying **get global score**
/5 blocks) that we created in step 2 into the left side of the **equal to** block and the
number **0** into the right side. The following screenshot shows the completed steps
plugged to the **if** statement:

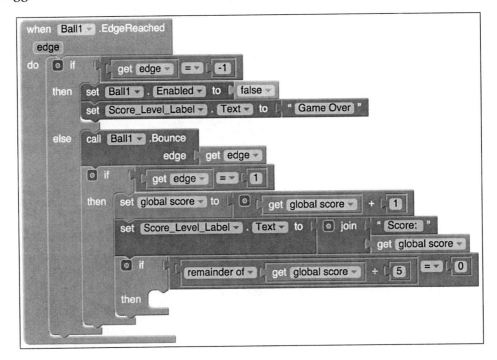

Blocks placed within the **then** part of an **if/then** statement are executed only when
the condition plugged to the **if** statement is true. In this case, when the score is a
multiple of 5 (that is, the whole remainder equals 0 and the if block evaluates to
be true), we would want to increase the speed. We need two blocks from the Ball1
drawer. The first block, **Ball1.Speed**, gives us the current value of **Ball1**'s speed
property. The second one, **set Ball1.Speed**, lets us change the speed.

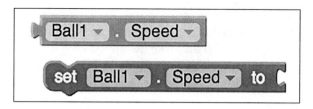

Since we want to increase the speed relative to the current speed, we will use both these blocks by:

1. Using **Ball1.Speed** to get the current speed.
2. Increasing the **Ball1.Speed** value by a small amount.
3. Using the result to set the new speed.

To complete these steps, drag an **add** block from the **Math** blocks and attach it to the **set Ball1.Speed** block. Insert the **Ball1.Speed** block into the opening on the left-hand side of the plus sign and a **number** Math block set to 2 (the small amount that we are increasing the speed by) in the opening on the right-hand side of the plus sign. This completes tasks 1, 2, and 3. Finally, we will place the block within the **then** block, as shown in the following screenshot:

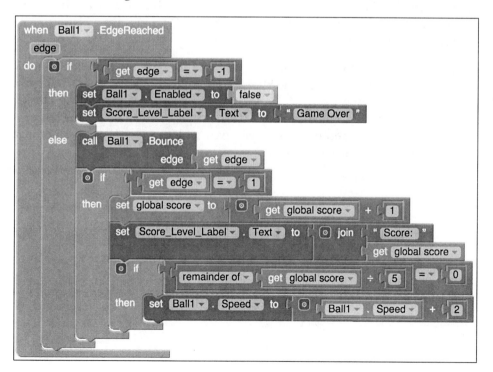

To summarize, whenever the user scores a point, the new score will be calculated. Then, the app will check to see whether the new score is a multiple of 5 or not. If it is indeed a multiple of 5, the app will increase the speed by a little bit to make the game harder. If the score is not a multiple of 5, nothing will change; the speed will remain the same.

We have completed coding the leveling part of our app! Can you think of what is still missing? We need to display the new level in the label!

Updating the score label to display the level

In our game, we have a label that displays the score or the words **"Game Over"**. Now that we have implemented levels as well, we also want to display the level within that label.

As shown in the following screenshot, we used the **join** block to join two pieces of information and display it in the label—the word **Score:** (there is a blank space after the colon) and the value of the score. Now that we want to display the level, we will add three more pieces of information to this **join** block. There is another blank space after the score (value), followed by the word **"Level: "** (there is also a blank space after the colon here), and finally the value of level.

To make room for these three new pieces of information, we need to add strings to the existing **join** block. Click on the blue square in the top left corner of the **join** block. This will open a pop-up window. Inside this popup, drag the **string** block from the top left corner into the **join** block on the right-hand side. Do this three times. Each time you add another **string**, you will see a new space appear in the **join** block below the **get global score** block.

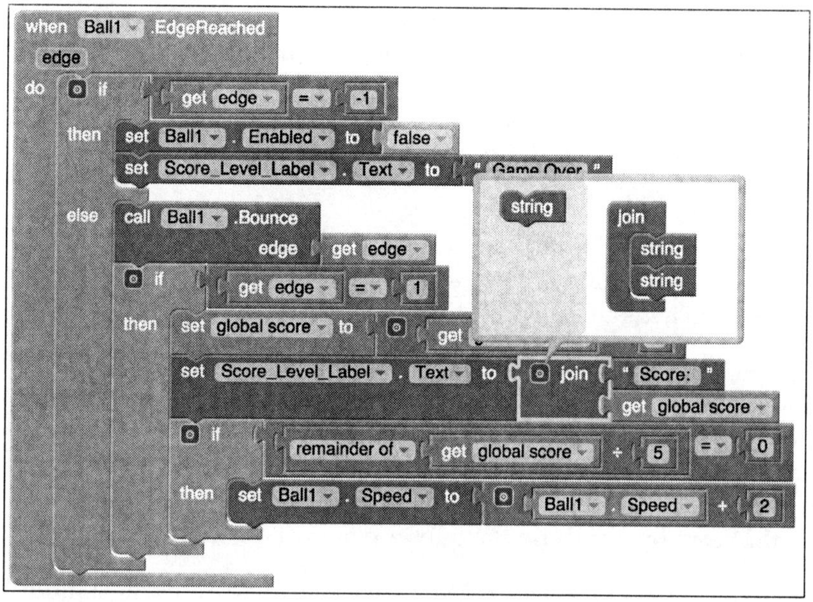

If you have done this correctly, there will be three empty slots, as shown in the following screenshot. Now, click anywhere outside the popup to close the pop-up menu.

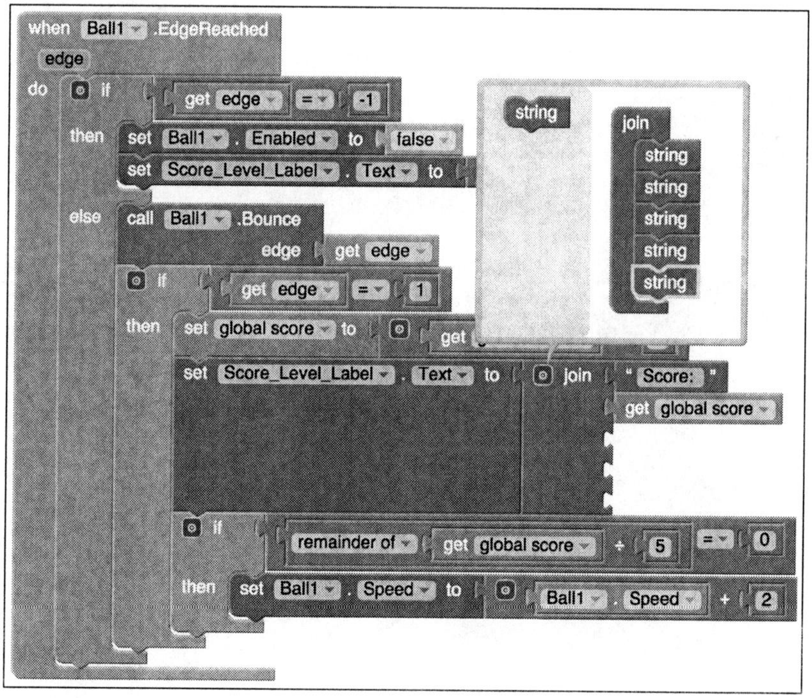

Now, we are ready to plug in the three new pieces of information related to the levels. Plug in a blank text box in the first open slot (the blank text block is the first block in **Text** block's drawer). Even though it seems like this contains a blank space, we must make one. Click inside the blank text and press your keyboard's spacebar to create a space. In the next empty slot, plug in another blank text block, and click and type in the word **Level:** with a space after the colon.

As you might have correctly guessed, the last piece of text we will plug into the **join** block is the level value. You might be wondering where this level value is going to come from. We will actually calculate this from the current score value.

When we implemented the levels, we assumed that an increase in score by 5 will trigger a level change. Hence, scores 0 to 4 correspond to level 0, scores 5 to 9 correspond to level 1, scores 10 to 14 correspond to level 2, and so on. We can use some math to calculate the level from the score. As you might have guessed, the math that we are going to use here is the quotient operation. More specifically, we will divide the score by 5 and use the quotient part to determine our levels.

To use the quotient block, go back to **Math** Blocks drawer and drag a **modulo** block. Then, click on the downward pointing triangle to change it to **quotient**. Copy a **get global score** block and plug it into the first open socket of the **quotient** block. Insert a Math **number** block into the second opening and change it to 5. The completed blocks are shown in the following screenshot:

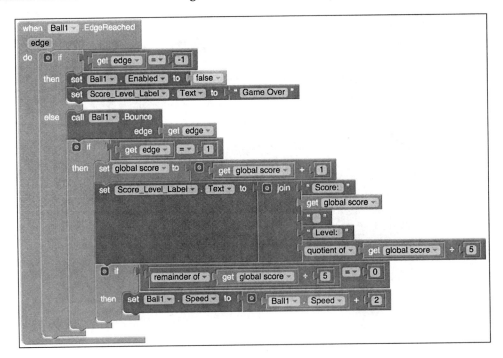

This is an ideal time to reconnect your mobile device to your Fling app. Your Label will now display both the score and the level, as shown in the following screenshot:

Updating the Reset button

Don't think that we have forgotten about our bug! Have you figured out what the bug is?" In the last chapter, we programmed the Reset button to move the ball to the top of the screen (y=2) and to a random x value. But, before the Play button starts the ball moving, it also moves the ball to a random x location. And the problem is, it isn't the same location that the Reset button previously set. So the ball moves once upon Reset and again on Play. We can fix this problem!" START A NEW PARAGRAPH Start it with "In addition to fixing the bug, we have some other updates to the Reset and Play buttons. Now that we have added scoring and leveling to our game, we need to edit the Reset button. There are several tasks related to resetting the game. They are as follows:

1. Stopping the ball's motion and resetting the position of the ball.
2. Resetting the score variable.
3. Updating the label used to display the score.

Another point to note is that we can't assume that the only reason a user presses Reset is because the ball hit the bottom edge and the game ended. We also have to think of the scenario of the user pressing the Reset button to stop the game.

To reset the position of the ball, we will reuse the **Ball1.MoveTo** block that we already coded in *Chapter 3, Navigating the App Inventor Platform*, when we created the **Play_Button.Click** event. When the user presses **Play** button, the ball will move to a random **x** coordinate between the value of **1** and the screen width.

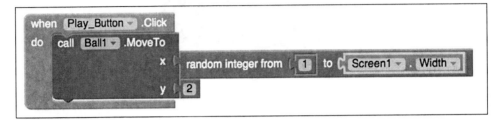

You may also recall in *Chapter 3, Navigating the App Inventor Platform*, that we programmed the **Reset** button to move the ball to a random integer between **1** and the screen width, as shown in the following screenshot:

As the app is currently programmed, the Reset button moves the ball to a random *x* position at the top of the screen and the Play button also moves the ball to a random *x* position at the top of the screen, but these two random positions are not the same. Imagine a scenario in which the ball hits the bottom edge and ends the game. A user presses Reset to move the ball back up to the top of the screen. It goes to a random *x* location. Then, when the user presses Play, the ball is again reset to a new random *x* location before it starts moving downward.

We first programmed the Play button to position the ball at the top of the screen, because the first time the game is played, the user wouldn't press the Reset button, but rather the Play button. However, after the game is played once, the user would press Reset and thus the Play button would no longer need to reposition the ball, since the Reset button will perform this function.

We want the Play button to let the ball start moving from the same location that the Reset button previously randomly selected. To do this, we need to program our app so that the Play button gets the ball's x location from the **Reset** button.

To make this Reset_Button and Play_Button communication happen, we will first create a variable called **randomX**. This variable will initially be set to **0**. Initializing a variable to some value (even if that value is not used later on) is important. Select the **initialize global name to** block from the **Variables** blocks drawer. Change the name to **randomX**. Select a number **Math** block and attach it, as shown in the following screenshot (note that this set of blocks stands on its own; it does not fit into the other event blocks):

After initializing the global variable, randomX, we can now use it for both our Reset and Play buttons. If you recall, when we programmed the Play_Button.Click event, we enabled the ball to start moving. We set the value of the set Ball1.Enabled block to true, as shown in the following screenshot:

```
when Play_Button .Click
do  call Ball1 .MoveTo
                      x   random integer from 1 to Screen1 . Width
                      y   2
    set Ball1 . Heading to  random integer from 200 to 340
    set Ball1 . Enabled to  true
```

So, for the **Reset** button, we want to disable the ball. And we do this by making the value **false**.

First, copy and paste the **set Ball1.Enabled** block; it will also copy and paste the attached **true** block. Simply click on the arrow to the right of the word **true** and you will be able to select **false**. This block disables the ball's movement. This was one of our goals, since the user will expect the game to stop when the Reset button is pressed.

Next, select the **set global randomX** block from the **Variables** block (it will be available as a choice in the blocks drawer, since we initialized the global variable, **randomX**). We will generate a random integer for the x coordinate and store it in this **randomX** variable. You know how to do this because we have already created the blocks to move the ball to a random x integer. Copy and paste the **random integer from to** blocks and add them to the **set global randomX to** block, as shown in the following screenshot. Once we set the global randomX variable to a random integer, we will use this variable in the **Call Ball1.MoveTo** block. The following screenshot shows how to generate a random number, store it in the variable (set **global randomX**), and then use this variable (get **global randomX**). This completes *Task 1*.

Tasks 2 and *Task 3* are relatively easy. Since the Reset button also resets the score to equal zero, we will also set the score variable to zero. To do this, we will copy and paste the **set global score** block from the **Ball1.EdgeReached** event and modify the right-hand side to simply be a Math number block of the value 0. For *Task 3*, we will simply copy and paste the **Score_Level_Label.Text** block that we created previously in this chapter. This block always updates the label using the latest value of the score and the level. Since we are resetting the score to 0 right before we execute this block, this block will correctly reset the label to show **0** for the score and the level.
(Note: blocks execute from top to bottom.)

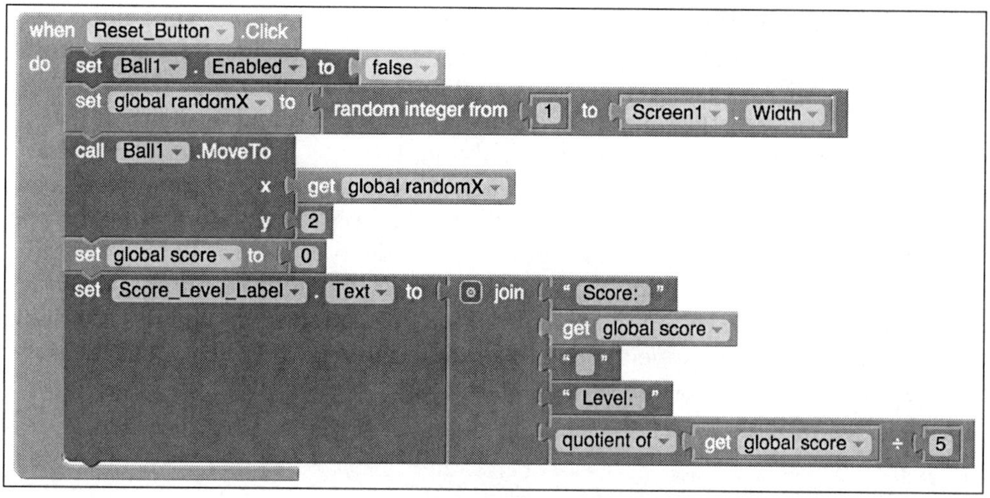

```
when  Reset_Button ▼ .Click
do   set  Ball1 ▼ . Enabled ▼  to   false ▼
     set  global randomX ▼  to    random integer from  [ 1 ]  to [ Screen1 ▼ . Width ▼ ]
     call  Ball1 ▼ .MoveTo
                        x [ get  global randomX ▼ ]
                        y [ 2 ]
     set  global score ▼  to  [ 0 ]
     set  Score_Level_Label ▼ . Text ▼  to  [ ⊗ join [ " Score: "
                                                       get  global score ▼
                                                       " ● "
                                                       " Level: "
                                                       quotient of ▼ [ get  global score ▼ ] ÷ [ 5 ] ]
```

Updating the Play button

When we built the Play button, the blocks resembled the following screenshot:

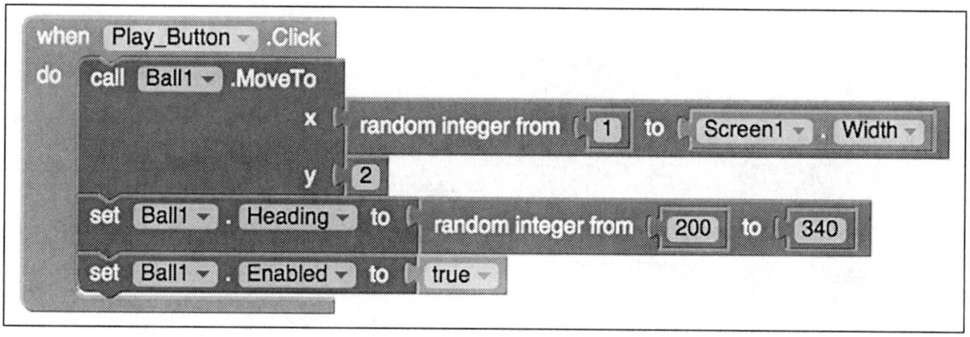

```
when  Play_Button ▼ .Click
do   call  Ball1 ▼ .MoveTo
                        x [ random integer from  [ 1 ]  to [ Screen1 ▼ . Width ▼ ] ]
                        y [ 2 ]
     set  Ball1 ▼ . Heading ▼  to  [ random integer from  [ 200 ]  to [ 340 ] ]
     set  Ball1 ▼ . Enabled ▼  to  [ true ▼ ]
```

But now, we want to redo the Play button blocks because we no longer want the Play button to set the ball's x random location. Instead, we want the Play button to get the location of the ball from the Reset button. This way, when the Play button is pressed, the ball will just begin moving from where it already is, having just been reset to the top of the screen by the Reset button between the very first time a user plays the game, the Play button will set the random location of the ball using the blocks we already programmed. Then the first time (and ensuing times) that the Reset button is pressed and sets the location of the ball at the top of the screen, we want the ball to start moving from that location when the Play button is pressed.

At this point, it might be obvious that we will use an **if/then/else** event block. The reasoning, however, is a little counter-intuitive. The only time the Play button determines the ball's x location is the very first time that the user plays the app. This is when the global variable, randomX, has the value of 0. Instead of saying if the global randomX is equal to 0, then do something, we are going to say if the **global randomX** is not equal to 0, then do something. We are going to program the blocks this way because there is only one time this won't happen. Every other time the app checks this information, the global randomX will indeed be a value between 1 and the screen width (as we coded in the Reset button). If the **global randomX** *is not equal to 0*, *then* move the ball to the global randomX location set by the Reset button. Otherwise (else), we will move the ball to a random integer between 1 and the screen width (this code will only occur once — the first time the user plays the Fling app).

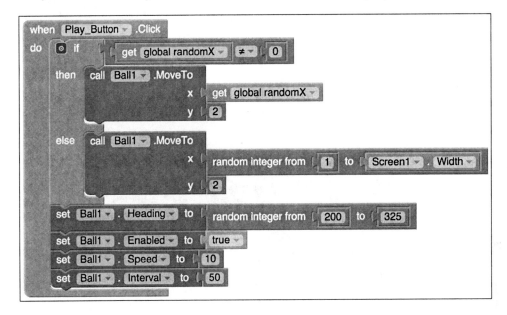

Summary

We hope you found this chapter to be challenging yet rewarding. You have learned how to take a simple app and make it more intermediate by adding more complex features and code. Each feature, scoring, fling capability, and level requires a lot of thought on how each would work and interact with each other. As you experienced, enabling scoring and leveling mechanisms required us to alter code in a variety of block locations. Similarly, we had to reexamine how our buttons functioned and reprogram the buttons. You will discover that this is a typical process in coding. Changing or adding one thing requires reevaluating how other things would work and interact. Also, this chapter demonstrates how much thought needs to go into planning an app. Earlier in this chapter we decided to update our Label from Score to Score_Level_label to reflect that it would be displaying the Score, Level and Game Over. If you don't take sufficient time to map out your app design on paper initially, then you will most likely end up having to do more re-working than you may have anticipated. Most programming efforts require coders to do some troubleshooting along the way, so don't be discouraged if you find that your app building includes many rewrites. But, you can avoid grand overhauls by really thinking through each aspect of your app's features ahead of time.

In the next chapter, we will begin working on an intermediate app, an event app to plan events, parties, or meetings.

5
Building an Event App

Now that we've successfully created a game app, let's try something new! In this chapter, you will learn to use more components and blocks—this time, to create an event app. This type of app is helpful to organize an event where you will gather a group of people for a specific activity, such as a party, book club, outing, or meeting. In building this type of app, you will learn how to do the following:

- Include images
- Create a navigation menu of buttons
- Add multiple screens
- Use multiple labels
- Set up a map feature

We are transitioning into a beginner-intermediate level of app-making, so you will discover that some features in this app require multiple steps. For example, in this chapter, we will be setting up the user interface for the RSVP form and the Guest List display, but we will actually be creating the database and coding the blocks for these in *Chapter 6, Introduction to Databases*.

As with any tutorial, this one will most probably spark creative ideas about other ways you could use these components or more features you may want to add to the app. Be sure to jot down your jolts of inspiration in a notebook when they occur. We recommend saving your app building ideas and concepts in one place. You will amass a valuable resource for when you finish the tutorials and embark out on your own app development.

User Interface for an event app

Sign into App Inventor by clicking on the **Create Apps** button on the App Inventor home page (`http://appinventor.mit.edu/explore/`) and logging into your Google account. Once you are in App Inventor, click on **Start new project** in the upper-left corner of the screen (the location is the same whether you are in the **Projects** view or in the **Designer** view). A pop-up window will appear (as shown in the following screenshot); type `EventApp` for the project name:

Create new App Inventor project
Project name: `EventApp`
Cancel   OK

Once you click on **OK**, you will be taken into the **Designer** view.

Setting the background image

In this chapter, you will gain experience in using the media tool to include images in your app. All the apps include some sort of artwork (logos, icons, photos, and so on), so learning to include image files will come in handy. We've decided to create a pool party for our EventApp tutorial, and to keep with the theme, we will set the background image for Screen1 to a water image. It is extremely important to note that you *cannot* use just any image, logo, or artwork from the Internet in your app. Artwork (this includes photography) is copyrighted, and if you use someone else's artwork without permission (and without paying for it), you will be violating copyright law. Thus, we are taking the time to explain how to find usable, free artwork. Google makes it easy to find artwork that is free to reuse or remix.

1. Type in the topic you are looking for in the Google search bar. In this case, we will type in **pool**. Press return on your keyboard or click on the blue magnifying glass icon next to the search bar.

2. Google will display the results. Below the search bar, you will see a horizontal list of options; click on **Images**.

3. To the far right of **Images**, click on **Search Tools**. This button will reveal a pop-up window with more options. They include the following:

   ° Not filtered by license (*do not use this option*)

   ° Labeled for reuse with modification

   ° Labeled for reuse

   ° Labeled for noncommercial reuse with modification

   ° Labeled for noncommercial reuse

4. The following screenshot displays the Google search options for our pool image search:

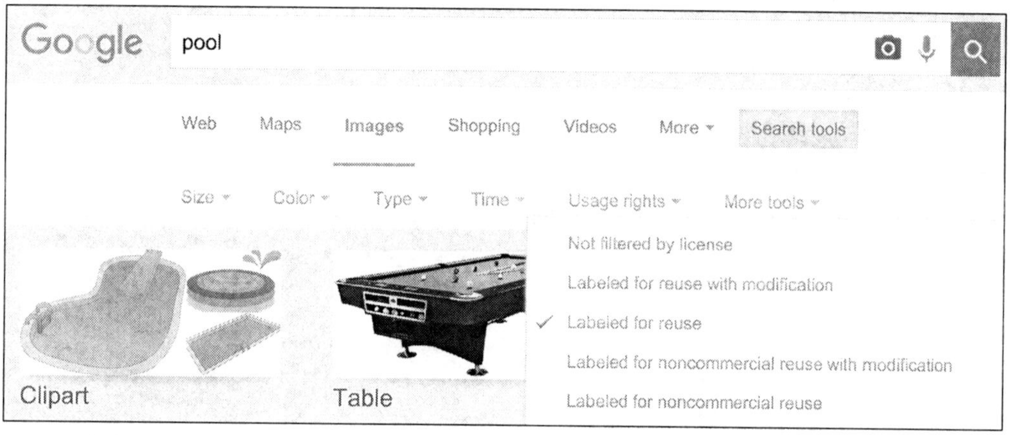

Selecting an option from the drop-down menu in this case, Labeled for reuse will filter the displayed results to only include images with a license for that particular category. Again, we cannot stress enough that it is good practice to pick images labeled for reuse. This way, you can use them commercially in case you ever decide to sell your app.

Here is a quick explanation of some helpful terms:

- **Free to use or share**: You are allowed to use or share the content if you do not alter it

- **Free to use, share, or modify**: You are allowed to use, share, or change the content

- **Commercially**: If you think you may ever want to sell an app that uses artwork from the Internet, make sure you choose artwork that is available for commercial use

You can also search online for *Creative Commons* images that come with many different licenses. Some photos require attribution, meaning that you are required to give the photographer credit by including the text: *photo by (and the name of the photographer)*. You do not have to give attribution if the artwork is free to use commercially or if it is considered in the public domain (free unrestricted use).

 For more detailed information on license types, visit `https://creativecommons.org/licenses/`. An especially interesting side note: the Creative Commons organization was cofounded by Hal Abelson, the creator of MIT App Inventor.

Once you find an image you like that is free to use, download it to your computer (by right-clicking on the image on a Windows machine or by clicking and holding down the **Option** key on a Mac). You will see a pop-up window. Click on **Save Image As...**. This will launch another pop-up window where you can rename the file to something that is descriptive or memorable and choose the location on your computer where you would like to save the image.

Once the image is saved on your computer, there are two methods to upload a photo: through the **Media** panel or through the **Properties** panel—steps for both are exactly the same. Note that the only way to delete media files is via the **Media** panel.

Since we will be adding a pool water image as the background image to our app, we will upload it to Screen1. When **Screen1** is highlighted, there will be an option in the **Properties** panel called **BackgroundImage**. Since our screen is empty, it will say **None**. When you click on the text **None**, a drop-down menu will appear, enabling you to upload an image, as shown in the following screenshot:

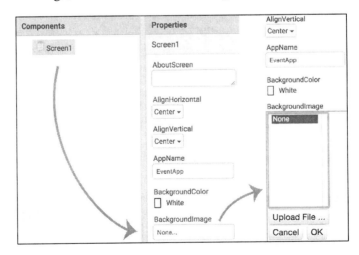

When you click on the **Upload File...** button, a pop-up window will appear, enabling you to choose an image from your computer. We named ours **Pool Image.png**:

Once you click on **OK**, the image name will appear on the drop-down menu in the **Properties** and **Media** panels and the actual image will appear on **Screen1** as the background image, as shown in the following screenshot (note: we named the image Pool Image.png; but when it was uploaded to App Inventor, it was assigned a new name: PoolImage.png with no spaces). If your photo isn't centered, you can always adjust the **AlignHorizontal** and **AlignVertical** properties by choosing **Center** from the drop-down menus, as shown in the following screenshot:

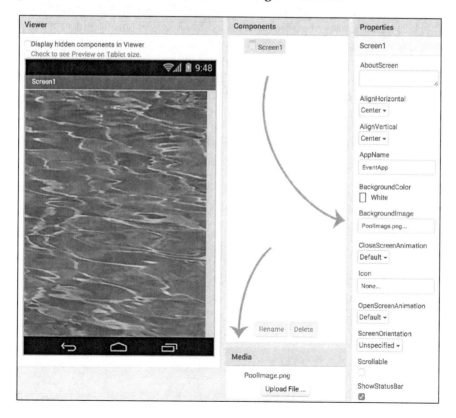

Adding an image component

Next, we will add another image to lay over the background image. We used Illustrator and Photoshop to create some artwork and saved it as a .png file. If you don't have these software programs, you can use free editors, such as Inkscape (Windows/Linux), Affinity Designer (Mac), or Gimp (multi-platform) to create artwork. You could make an image similar to ours or a new design, or find Creative Commons image online.

In the far left column in the Designer, in the **User Interface** palette drawer, choose the **Image** Component and drag it to the **Viewer**. You will notice that a small image component icon sits in the upper-left corner of the Viewer. We want to center it. There are two ways to do this:

- Click on **Screen1** in the **Components** panel, and in the **Properties** panel, select **Center** from both the **AlignHorizontal** and **AlignVertical** drop-down lists.

- Since we are going to be adding many components to our home screen, we are going to walk you through a more complex method that requires an extra component. Go to Layout drawer and drag out the **VerticalArrangement** component onto the **Viewer**. Notice how it sits below the **Image** Component icon. Click on the **Image Component** icon and drag it into the VerticalArrangement box. In the **Components** panel, select **VerticalArrangement** and go to the **Properties** panel. In both the **Height** and **Width** options, select **Fill Parent** from the drop-down menu and click on **OK** for each. You will see the VerticalArrangement component expand to fill the screen. Still in the **Properties** panel, go to the **AlignVertical** and **AlignHorizonal** options and select **Center** from each drop-down menu. Notice how the Image component is now centered in the Viewer on Screen1.

Next we will change the name of the Image component. Go to the **Components** panel and select **Image1**. Once it is highlighted, click on **Rename** at the bottom of the panel to see a pop-up window where you can enter a new name, Pool Party Message. Click on **OK**:

Note that App Inventor replaces the spaces with underscores, so the Image component name will now appear as **Pool_Party_Message** in the **Components** panel. Now, we will upload the actual image for the Image component. With **Pool_ Party_Message** highlighted, go to the **Properties** panel and click on **None** under **Picture** to open the **Upload File** dialogue. Choose the image you want to use (we named our image in a similar way: `PoolPartyMessage.png`) and click on **OK**. Notice that the image name appears in the Properties panel under Picture and in the Media panel, and the actual image is displayed over our background image on Screen1 in the Viewer, as shown in the following screenshot:

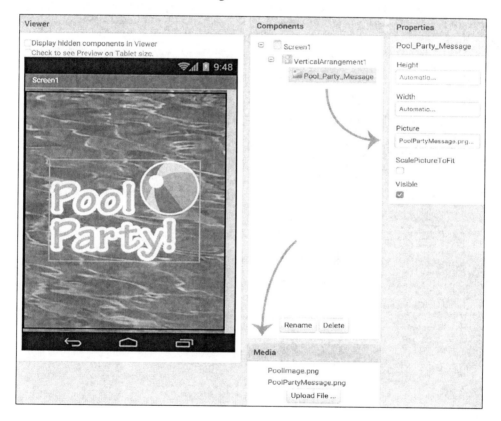

As a mobile apps user, you may have noticed that apps have some sort of navigation bar. We will build ours across the bottom of the screen by adding five buttons: **Home**, **Info**, **RSVP**, **Guests**, and **Map**.

Adding buttons

We are going to place our buttons within a **HorizontalArrangement** component. Drag it from the same place you found VerticalArrangement (the Layout drawer drawer) and drop it underneath **VerticalArrangment** that currently exist on the **Viewer**. You can double-check that **HorizontalArrangement** is indeed below and not within VerticalArrangement by seeing that their names align in the Components panel column, as shown in the following screenshot. The list of components shows that Pool_Party_Message is indented so that it is indeed within the VerticalArrangement1 component, but HorizontalArrangement1 is not. Next, set the properties for **HorizontalArrangement1** to match those indicated in the following screenshot:

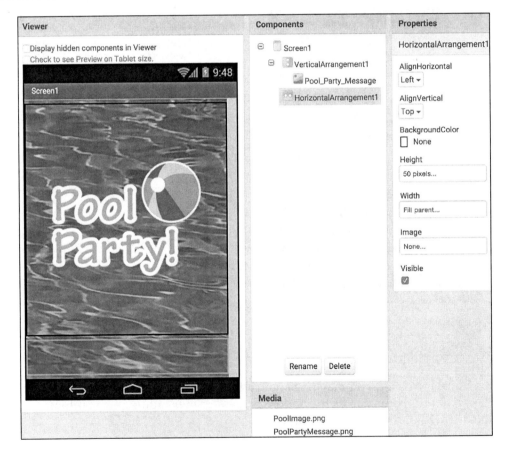

Go to the **User Interface** palette, drag out a **Button**, and place it inside **HorizontalArrangement** in the **Viewer**. Repeat this step four more times. You will now have five buttons at the bottom of the screen, as shown in the following screenshot. Since we already set the height of HorizontalArrangement to 50 pixels, you can set the **Height** property of all the buttons to **Fill parent**. This way, they will stretch only to the height of 50 pixels. Do the same for the **Width** property and all the buttons will automatically size evenly across the width of the screen:

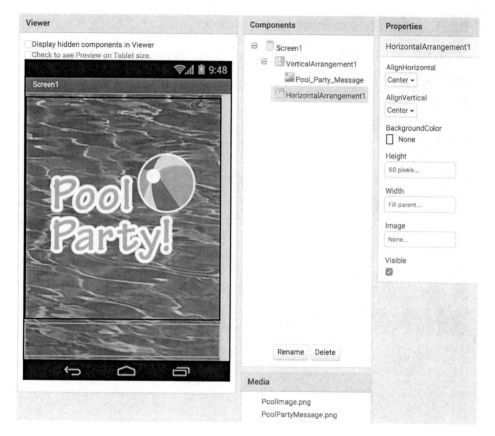

Click on **Button1** in the **Components** panel and rename it to **HomeButton**. In the **Properties** panel, change **BackgroundColor** to **None**, check **Enabled** and **FontBold**, and set **FontSize** to 14. Under **Text**, type **Home**, and select **Center** for **TextAlignment** and **Black** for **TextColor**, as shown in the following screenshot:

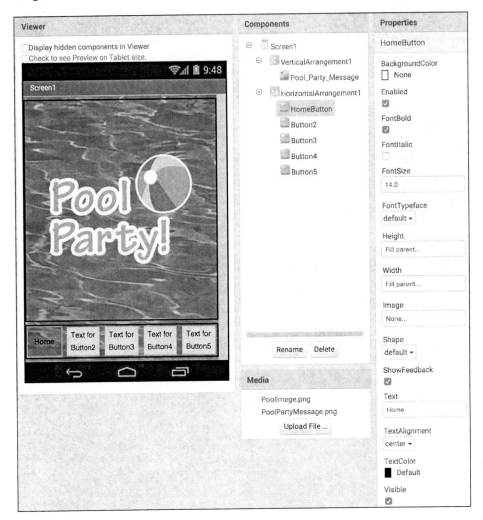

Repeat these steps for all of the other buttons, renaming the buttons and changing the text on the buttons to reflect the names indicated in the following screenshot. Set all of the buttons' **TextColor** to **White**. We are using different colors to aid navigation. When the user is on the **Home** screen, he or she will see the **Home** button's **TextColor** in black, while the other buttons will be white, as shown in the next screenshot. When we build the next screen (**Info**), we will make the **Info** button's text black, and change the **Home** text button to white, like the others:

Here's an ideal example of why you would want to always take advantage of the live development environment and monitor changes you make to your app on your mobile device. The screenshot on the left-hand side is from the **Viewer** in the **Designer** window. It shows the home screen (**Screen1**) with the background image, the graphic, and the bottom menu bar we just built. If you relied only on this view from your computer screen, you might attempt to respace the buttons because it looks like the right button is cut off.

But if you were to look at this same view on your mobile device, you would see the screenshot on the right-hand side with all the buttons fitting evenly across the screen.

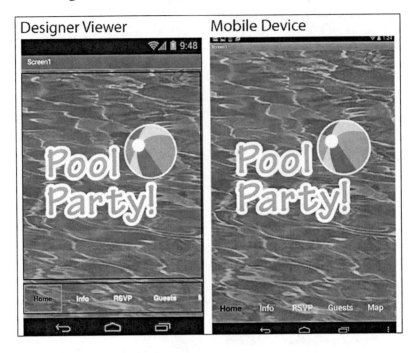

Adding the ActivityStarter

Our app will feature a map, because anytime you host an event, guests will need to know the address and it is helpful to provide the location via GPS. For the EventApp app to launch Google Maps when a user presses the Map button, we will use the ActivityStarter Component. Go to the **Designer**, and in the **Connectivity** Palette, drag **ActivityStarter** onto the **Viewer** and notice how it drops down below the **Viewer** (see the following screenshot) unlike all of the other components we have used so far. This is because **ActivityStarter** is a nonvisible component; the user won't see it on the screen or even know that they have launched it:

For the app to launch the correct map, you will need to input some instructions in the **Properties** panel. Insert the following text into the blank text boxes beneath each property heading `Action`, `ActivityClass`, `ActivityPackage`, and `DataUri`, as follows:

- **Action**: `android.intent.action.VIEW`
- **ActivityClass**: `com.google.android.maps.MapsActivity`
- **ActivityPackage**: `com.google.android.apps.maps`
- **DataUri**: `http://maps.google.com/mapsq=1600+Amphitheatre+Parkway+Mountain+View+CA`

You might be wondering what all of these properties mean. The **ActivityPackage** property tells ActivityStarter what package to launch (in the Android programming jargon, the app files are called packages). Every Android app consists of one or more activities. Think of these activities as main parts of the app. The **ActivityClass** property mentions specifically which activity of the Maps app to start. The **Action** property provides more details about the activity that is being launched. Finally, the **DataUri** property specifies the web location that the map is pointing to. The first part of the URL, `http://maps.google.com/maps?q=`, basically means that we are querying Google Maps (the `q` stands for query) and the second part of the URL specifies the exact location we are looking for. In URLs, blank spaces are not allowed, so the conventional format is to replace all the black spaces with plus signs. Thus, when we specify the address of our pool party (is fictionally at the Google headquarters in Mountain View, CA), all the blank spaces between different words will be replaced by plus signs, as shown in the previous list under the **DataUri** property heading.

When creating your own event app with a different location, you will use the same information for **Action**, **ActivityClass**, and **ActivityPackage**, but for the **DataUri** property, you will insert your address after the equals sign (`http://maps.google.com/maps?q=`). Remember to replace all the spaces in your address with plus signs.

Following is a sample of what your screen should resemble. Because the text boxes on your screen are small, it will not display the full information without scrolling the cursor to the right using the arrow keys:

Properties

ActivityStarter1

Action

android.intent.action.VIEV

ActivityClass

com.google.android.maps

ActivityPackage

com.google.android.apps

DataType

DataUri

http://maps.google.com/r

Adding screens

We currently have our home screen called Screen1 (because App Inventor does not allow you to rename Screen1). We will now add three more screens; each one will be associated with a button. Above the **Viewer** and below **Projects** in the top menu bar, you will see a row of three buttons: **Screen1** (our current screen), **Add Screen...**, and **Remove Screen**, which is grayed out, as shown in the following screenshot:

Click on the **Add Screen** button and a pop-up window will ask you to input the new screen name. Type Info_Screen as shown in the following screenshot. Click on **OK**:

Repeat the same procedure to add two more screens and name them **RSVP_Screen** and **GuestList_Screen**. Now, all of your screens will appear in the drop-down menu under the first menu button, and you can navigate between screens by selecting a different one. The next screenshot shows the name **Screen1** on the button to indicate the name of the screen that is currently open:

Once you have added the additional screens, you will need to recreate the user interface for them. This means that, for each screen, you will add some of the same elements you added to Screen1: the pool image as the background image, a VerticalArrangement, a HorizontalArrangement, and five buttons. Note that it is vital to rename the five buttons to the exact same names as on Screen1 because we will be programming each button with the same name to do the same thing (to open its appropriate screen) and if a button is misnamed on one of the screens, it won't work (note that we are referring to the actual button names, not the text that appears on the buttons). Also, remember to make the text of all the buttons white, except for the button of the screen that you have open (that is, when GuestList_Screen is open, the Guests button text should be black; when RSVP_Screen is open, the RSVP button text should be black, and so on).

Programming the blocks

Now that we've designed most of the user interface of the Event app, we will switch to the Blocks editor to program our app. Click on the **Blocks** button in the upper-right corner of the Designer. You will find that throughout the building of this app (as with any app), you will go back and forth between the Designer and Blocks editor.

Navigating between screens and launching maps

In the Blocks editor, we will code the navigation buttons to launch the appropriate screen. For example, when the user presses the Info button, we want the app to open Info_Screen.

Screen1

In the Blocks Editor, make sure you are on Screen1 by verifying that Screen1 (and not one of the other screens) displays on the menu button. In the **Blocks** palette under **HorizontalArrangement**, you will see a list of the buttons that you just created in the Designer. (Notice how the button names are indented underneath HorizontalArrangement, this is a visual cue to remind you that they are contained within the HorizontalArrangement Component.) If you don't see all of the buttons displayed in the Palette, click on the plus sign to the left of HorizontalArrangement, it will toggle to a minus sign and display those items (in this case, 5 buttons) within.

- Click on **InfoButton** to reveal the blocks drawer and choose the first gold block **when InfoButton.Click**.

- Under the **Built-in** blocks, click on the gold **Control** blocks and scroll down to the **open another screen screenName** block. Insert this block into the **when InfoButton.Click** block.

- Add a blank pink **Text** block to it and type `Info_Screen` into the blank. Connect it to the **open another screen screenName** block.

- Repeat these steps for **RSVPButton** and **GuestsButton**.

For MapButton, we won't be opening another screen; instead we will be launching the ActivityStarter (that we have already set to open Google Maps), as follows:

- In the **MapButton** drawer, select the first block, when **MapButton.Click**.

- In the **ActivityStarter1** blocks drawer, select the purple **call ActivityStarter1. StartActivity** block. Connect the two blocks together.

- The following screenshot shows all of the previous steps:

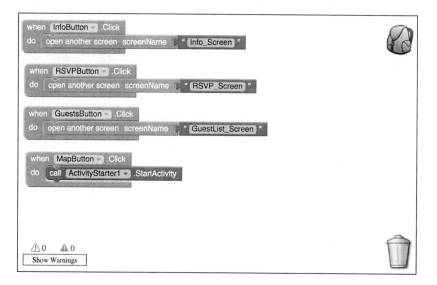

Sharing blocks between screens using the Backpack

If you think about it, all the buttons on all the screens will do the same thing. Instead of rebuilding the exact same sets of blocks for all of the other screens, we can use the Backpack tool. There is a little backpack icon in the upper-right corner of the blocks Viewer, as shown in the earlier screenshot. This tool enables you to share blocks between screens and projects (note that the Backpack empties when you sign out).

There are two ways to add blocks to the Backpack. They are as follows:

- You can drag the blocks directly to the Backpack (the simplest method).

- Or, you can right-click on block you want to add (similar to copying or pasting blocks, right-clicking to add blocks to the Backpack, will add all attached blocks). For example, right-click on the **when InfoButton.Click** block (or on a Mac, click on the control button on the keyboard while clicking on the event block) and a drop-down list will appear, as shown in the following screenshot. Select the fifth option, **Add to Backpack**; this will add the three blocks in this set (if you have your computer's sound on, you will hear an indicator sound).

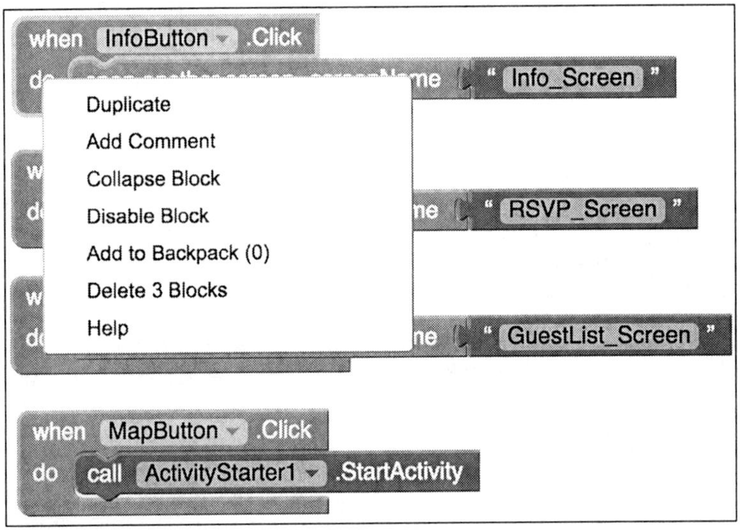

The first time you do this the number in the parenthesis in the drop-down list will be 0 (as shown in the preceding screenshot). But after you add the first set of blocks to the Backpack and repeat the step for the next set of blocks, the number will increase. This number lets you know how many times you have added blocks to the Backpack.

Add the three other block sets to the **Backpack**, in the method you choose. After adding the blocks, click on the Backpack to reveal the four block sets you have added, as shown on the right-hand side of the following screenshot. Click on any white space in the **Viewer** to close the Backpack:

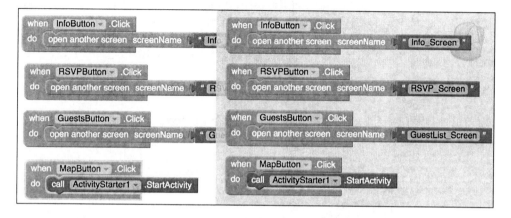

Now we can switch screens and retrieve our Backpack blocks. Click on the **Screen1** button above the **Viewer** to choose another screen from the drop-down list. Select **Info_Screen**.

If you think about it, we only need three of the four sets of blocks we added to the **BackPack**. We don't need the **InfoButton** blocks because we are currently on the **Info** screen, so we don't want the **InfoButton** to do anything. *To make a button not active or not do anything, we simply don't create any blocks (code) for it.*

Adding blocks from the Backpack works in exactly the same way as adding blocks from a drawer. Click on **Backpack** to reveal the selection of blocks you've added and click on the **RSVPButton** block. You will see that they those blocks appear on the **Viewer**. Repeat the steps to add the **GuestsButton** and the **MapButton** blocks from the Backpack.

We didn't need to create the **HomeButton** blocks when we were on **Screen1** because that is essentially the Home screen. But, we do need to activate the Home Button on other screens so users can navigate back to Screen1 (or Home). let's do that now that we are on the "Info_Screen. Copy and paste any event block on the screen and then click on the gold arrow to the right of the button name. It will reveal a drop-down list of all the buttons; choose **HomeButton**. Change the text in the pink Text block to **Screen1**. Your blocks for **Info_Screen** should look as like the following image. Repeat the same steps to add the Home Button blocks to the RSVP_Screen and the GuestList_Screen::

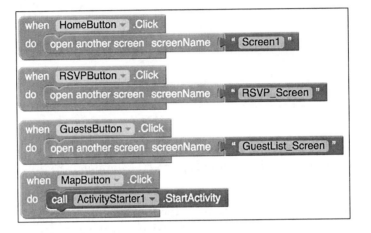

Adding text to screens

The purpose of **Info_Screen** is for the organizer (you) to provide guests with information about the event. This screen would display static text, but it could easily be updated. Let's switch back to the **Designer**.

An easy way to add text to a screen is with a **Label**. (Alternatively, you could also create the text on your computer using Photoshop or Gimp (or another design tool) and save it as an image file (JPG or PNG) and upload it to App Inventor using the Media tool). You will find the Label component in the **User Interface** drawer. We are going to create eight lines of text, so drag a Label onto the **Viewer** and repeat this seven more times. In the **Properties** panel, type your information in the text box under **Text**. You can copy our formatting for font, color, and layout, as shown in the following screenshot, or design your own:

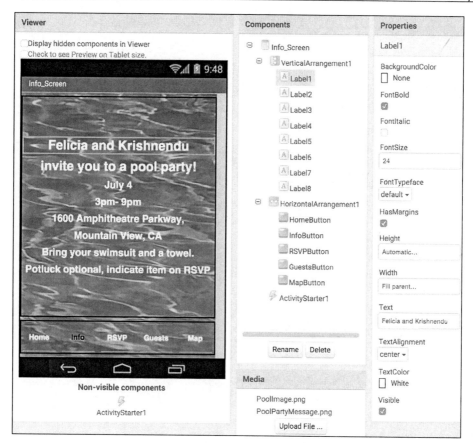

Summary

You have completed the first part of setting up an event app. In this chapter, you have learned how to find usable images online and how to use one as a background image on multiple screens. You also learned how to add artwork from a computer over a background image. You created a button navigation bar, coded buttons to open other screens, used the Backpack tool to copy blocks from one screen to another, entered informational text using labels, and did the setup for launching Google Maps.

In the next chapter, we will concentrate mostly on creating a database for all of the data we will be collecting—the guests' names, the number of attendees, and the potluck items. To do this, we will teach you to use Google Fusion Tables and how to create an RSVP form and a guest list display using **ListView**. We are halfway toward completing a very practical app that you can use for multiple purposes. And, the skills you are learning will prove instrumental for any and all future app-making endeavors.

Introduction to Databases

6

Now that we've successfully created the first part of the Event app, it is time to make it more functional. In this chapter, we will build onto our Event app by adding code that will enable guests to respond to the invitation by sending an RSVP (*répondez s'il vous plaît—please reply*, in French). The app will aggregate all the data and display a guest list so that both guests and party organizers can see who is attending.

In order for the app to collect all the RSVP data from individuals in a central repository, we will have to use an online database. App Inventor has built-in support for three online databases, TinyWebDB, and Google Fusion Tables (which we will use).

Both, TinyWebDB and Google Fusion Tables have their limitations in aggregating data. TinyWebDB, while easy to use, is not secure. This means that anyone has access to the database, could by mistake (or on purpose), delete or change the data that is collected. On the other hand, Google Fusion Tables is secure, but is more complicated to use. In order to integrate Fusion Tables into our app, while keeping the design of the app relatively simple, we had to make some tradeoffs. The learning objective is to introduce you to the process of building a database with a relatively simple app. But, as you will discover, the resulting app is challenging to disseminate to a broad public audience. At the time of publication for this book, another App Inventor database alternative, FirebaseDB was under development. We will offer updates about the adoption of FirebaseDB as it becomes available. You can check the supplementary materials on both the Packt Publishing and MIT App Inventor websites for new information about FirebaseDB.

In this chapter you will learn:

- How to create a Google Fusion Table
- How to establish Google API credentials
- How to set up an RSVP form
- How to push data from an App Inventor app into a Google Fusions Table

- How to request and receive data from a Google Fusion Table into an App Inventor app
- How to display a guest list

Creating a database

In this app, invitees will send an RSVP to let the party organizer (and other guests) know whether or not they can attend an event. So, naturally, we will have to include a mechanism to collate all of that distributed information into one central place. To achieve this, we will create an online database using a Google Fusion Table. In professional programming, this aspect is often referred to as creating the backend.

Creating a Google Fusion Table

To create a Google Fusion Table, go to the `https://drive.google.com` website on your computer and click on the big red button on the top-left side of the screen labeled **NEW**. Scroll down the list of options and select **More** and select **Google Fusion Tables**:

If you have never used Google Fusion Tables before, chances are, when you click on **More**, you will not see the **Google Fusion Tables** option listed. If this is the case, select the last option with the plus sign, **Connect more apps**. A pop-up window will appear with a lot of apps that you can connect to your Google Drive. You should see a view similar to the following screenshot. At the top left of this pop-up window you will see a button that by default shows the word **All**. This button lets you filter the apps into various categories. Click on it and select the second option, **By Google**, from the drop-down menu, as shown in the following screenshot:

Now, you will see a list of all Google-created apps as shown on the right-hand side of the preceding screenshot. Find the Google Fusion Tables app in the list and click on it. After doing so, the next time you click the red **NEW** button in `https://drive.google.com` and select **More**, Google **Fusion Tables** will appear as an option.

When you create a new Fusion Table, you will be given the option to create an empty table (along with some other options). For our purpose, select **Create empty table**.

Next, we will make the format of the table suitable for our app. First, rename the table to give it a meaningful name. Click on the current table name, which is **New Table**, in the top left corner. This will open a **Table information** window. Give your table a descriptive name such as EventApp Table and hit the **Save** button:

We will need to make further modifications to the table before it is ready to be used as the backend of our Event app. By default, a blank row is inserted in Fusion Tables. We want our table to be completely empty. To clear out the table, select the **Edit** tab on the top left corner of the screen, below the table name. You will see a **Delete all rows** option; click on it and confirm that you want to delete all rows:

EventAppTable

Edited at 5:49 PM

| File | Edit | Tools | Help | Rows 1 ▾ | Cards 1 | Map of Location | ➕ |

Add row

Edit row

Duplicate row

Delete selected row

Delete all rows

Change columns

Delete all rows?

You're about to permanently delete all rows of data in this table. This cannot be undone.

Delete all rows   Cancel

Now that we have a clean table, we need to decide what columns to use. For this Event app, we want to know who is coming (the name of the guest), how many people that person is bringing (the number of guests), and what items that guest is bringing to the party (potluck). This information is going to be used by the organizer to plan the party.

Each of these three pieces of information will be saved in a column on the Fusion Table. Four columns are automatically included when a Fusion Table is created. Since we only need three columns, we are going to delete one of the four default columns and modify the other three.

The **Edit** tab that you clicked to delete all the rows and clean up the table also contains another option called **Change columns**. We will use that options several times now to make all the changes to the columns. The default column names are **Text**, **Number**, **Location**, and **Date**. We will change them to **Guest Names**, **NumGuests**, and **ItemsBringing**.

To change the first column to **Guest Names**, click on the Edit tab and select the **Change columns** option and you will see the following screenshot. The first column is selected by default (the gray background on the left panel indicates it is active). Change the **Column name** to **Guest Names**. This column is already configured to save **Text** data (the **Type** option), hence we do not need to make any changes here:

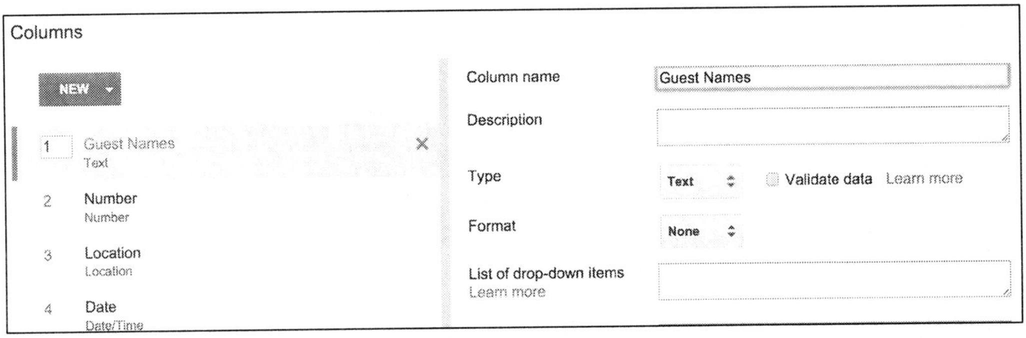

Now that we have changed the first column, we will do the same to the second column. Select the second column (currently called **Number**). Once you click on it, the background will become gray. Now change the **Column name** to **NumGuests**. Since, this column is already configured to store numbers, we do not need to make any changes here:

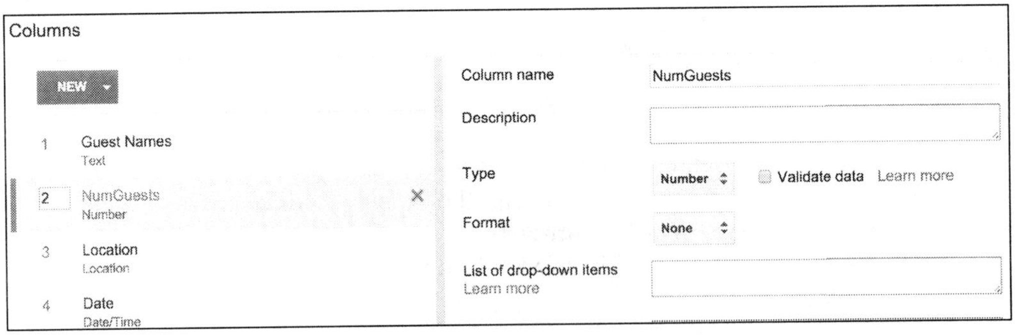

Next, we need to rename the third column (currently called **Location**). Just like the previous examples, select that column and change the name to **ItemsBringing**. By default this column is preconfigured to store **Location** data. We actually want to store **Text** data (items that guests will bring). So we need to change the datatype. When you click on **Location** (the **Type** option), a drop-down menu will appear as shown in the following screenshot. Select the **Text** option.

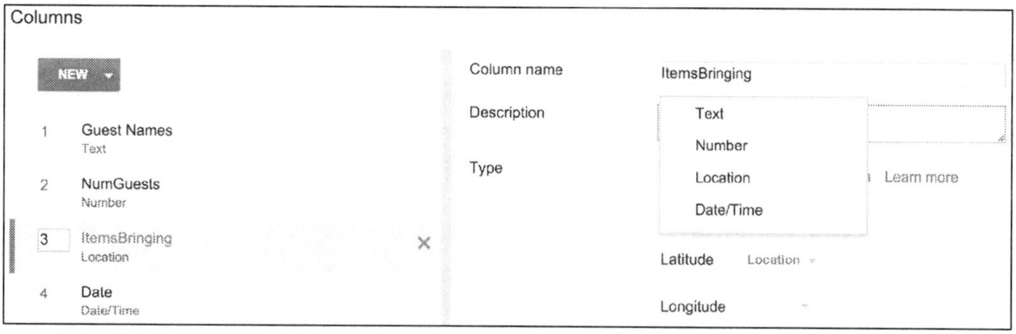

Finally, since we need only three columns, we will delete the fourth column by hovering over the fourth column to make it active (gray) and clicking on the x next to it (as shown in the following screenshot) and confirming the deletion in the pop-up box:

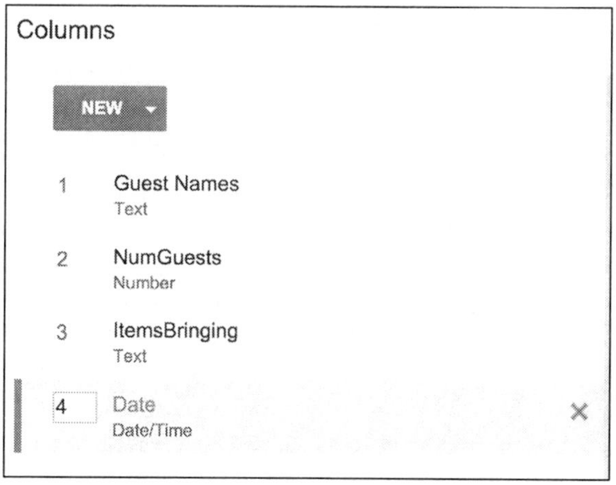

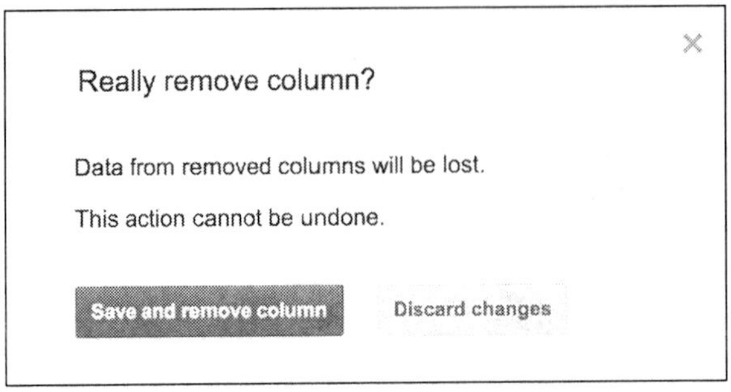

Really remove column?

Data from removed columns will be lost.

This action cannot be undone.

Save and remove column   Discard changes

Now that the table is ready to be used, click on the **File** tab in the upper left corner and select **About this table** from the drop-down menu.

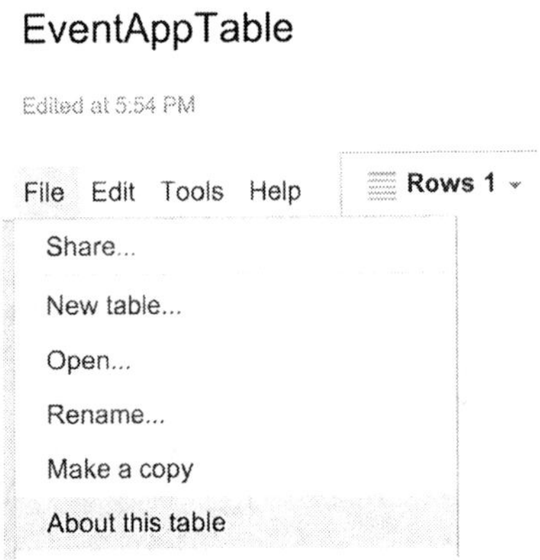

EventAppTable

Edited at 5.54 PM

File   Edit   Tools   Help   **Rows 1** ⌄

Share...

New table...

Open...

Rename...

Make a copy

About this table

Another page will open with various details of the table. Note the information given in the very last piece of information, the **Id**, as shown in the following screenshot. Double-click on the alphanumeric string to highlight it, copy/paste it in another place on your computer, such as a Notepad file or an empty document. (You may have to use your browser's copy/paste feature to do this, as keyboard shortcuts may not work. You can find copy/paste under the **Edit** menu heading at the top of your browser window.) You will use this **Id** in the App Inventor app to push/pull data to/from this table:

About this table

Name	EventAppTable
Visibility and reuse	Private Only people explicitly granted permission can access. Sign-in required Download allowed
Reuse license	Unknown
Protected map layer	Maps client ID not set up Set up now
Id	1Tcaw4l7j29YqrBaifiLEJeVgDJZRIfDufzpuQY3f

Done	Edit table information

We will make one small final change to the Fusion Table (to its **Sharing** settings) but, we are not ready to do that just yet. So keep the Fusion Table window open and start working with App Inventor in the separate browser window.

Designing the RSVP screen

For our app, we are asking the invited guests to provide their names, the total number of guests, and the food or drink to share at the potluck. Once a guest presses the **Send RSVP** button, something magical will happen. We will push all the data from the app to the Fusion Table that we created.

Creating the GUI in the designer window

In *Chapter 5, Building an Event App* we created the RSVP_Screen and now we will build the GUI (Graphical User Interface) that the guests will use. Navigate to the RSVP screen in the **Designer** window. The screen is empty except for the background pool image and the navigation buttons that we added along the bottom.

Since you have already gained experience adding various components in the previous chapters, we are pretty confident about your abilities. Of course, we will help specify which components to use! The guest provides three pieces of data here: the name, the number of guests, and the item to bring. We will place all the components related to these three pieces of data within a VerticalArrangement for a streamlined look. Hence, the first component to add is: **VerticalArrangement**. Drag it to the **Viewer** and set its **Height** and **Width** properties to **Fill parent**.

To collect the first piece of data, the name, add a **Label** and below that a **Textbox** by dragging them onto the Vertical Arrangement in the **Viewer**. Rename the **Label** to `NameLabel` and change the **BackgroundColor** property to **Dark Gray**. Check the **FontBold** property and change the **Text** property to **Name**.

Similarly, rename the **Textbox** to `NameTextBox`. Change the **Width** property to **Fill parent**. Type **Enter your first and last name** for the **Hint** property.

For the second piece of data, the number of guests, add a **Label** and another component called **ListPicker** (found just below the **Label** component in the **User Interface** palette). Drag the Components onto the VerticalArrangement underneath the Label and Textbox. Rename this Label to `GuestsLabel`. Change the **BackgroundColor** property to **Dark Gray**, check the **FontBold** property and change the **Text** property to **Number of guests (including you)**.

We will use the ListPicker Component to track the number of people attending when a guest submits an RSVP. The ListPicker is a button that, when clicked, opens up a list of items from which a user can select. Rename the **ListPicker** to `NumGuestListPicker`. We will make just two changes to the **ListPicker** properties. Put `1,2,3,4,5,6,7` as the **ElementsFromString** property. These are the items what we want displayed when the user clicks the **NumGuestListPicker**. We are assuming the number of guests (including the person who is completing the RSVP) is in the range 1-7. You can add more or fewer guest options as you wish.

Just remember that the comma-separated numbers that you specify are the options that the users will be able to select from. Finally, make the **Selection** property **1**. This means that, if the user does not choose a number from the **NumGuestListPicker**, the default value of 1 will be used to count the user who sent the RSVP.

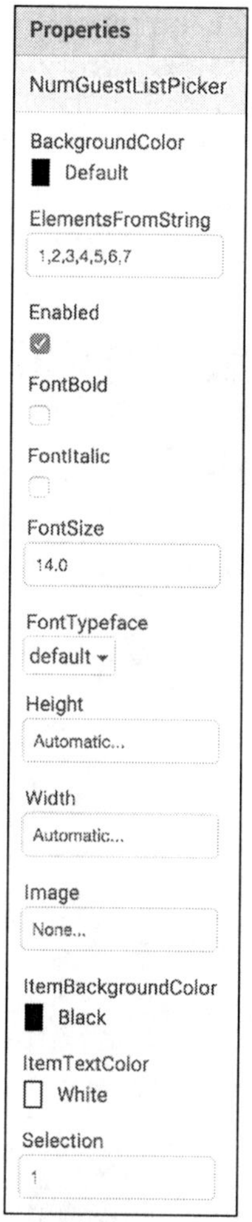

Properties

NumGuestListPicker

BackgroundColor
■ Default

ElementsFromString
1,2,3,4,5,6,7

Enabled
☑

FontBold
☐

FontItalic
☐

FontSize
14.0

FontTypeface
default ▾

Height
Automatic...

Width
Automatic...

Image
None...

ItemBackgroundColor
■ Black

ItemTextColor
☐ White

Selection
1

Finally, we will add a **Button** and rename it to `SendRSVPButton`. The user will click this button to send the RSVP after completing the form. Just as we did for the labels, make the **BackgroundColor** dark gray, and insert **Send RSVP** as the **Text** property.

Next, drag the **FusiontablesControl** component from the **Storage Palette** drawer to the Viewer. (Notice how the **FusiontablesControl1** component drops down below the **Viewer**, because it is a non-visible component.) After you have added all the components, the RSVP_Screen will resemble the following screenshot:

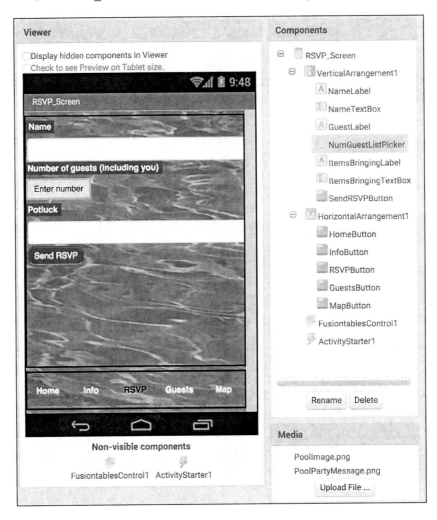

This completes the GUI for the RSVP_Screen. In professional programming lingo, this is also called creating the frontend.

Setting up Google Authentication

Fusion Tables is software that Google has designed. For various security- and privacy-related issues, Google only wants verified software to send/receive data to/from Fusion Tables. Hence, we need to establish our identity before our Event App can exchange data with Google Fusion Tables. In this section, we will describe how to create Google service-level authentication to establish this credential.

To establish the service-level authentication credentials, follow these instructions:

1. Go to `https://console.developers.google.com/` and log in with your Google account if necessary. On the **Getting started** page, click on the **Use Google APIs** button as shown in the following screenshot:

The acronym API stands for **Application Programming Interface**. To describe it in a very simple manner, an API defines a way for computers to interact with websites (essentially for software programs to interact). Developers at companies like Twitter, Facebook, and Google create protocols for their software to enable other programs to communicate with it. In this case App Inventor will be communicating with the Google Fusion Tables API.

2. You will be prompted to create a new project that uses APIs. Name your project **Event App Project**. Make the selections shown in the following screenshot, and click on **Create**:

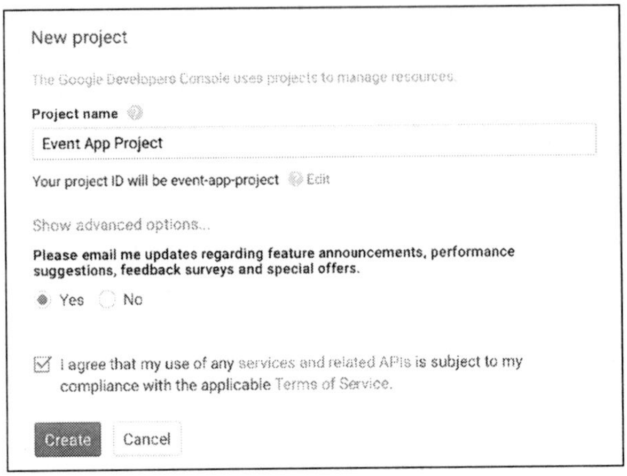

New project

The Google Developers Console uses projects to manage resources.

Project name

Event App Project

Your project ID will be event-app-project Edit

Show advanced options...

Please email me updates regarding feature announcements, performance suggestions, feedback surveys and special offers.

◉ Yes ○ No

☑ I agree that my use of any services and related APIs is subject to my compliance with the applicable Terms of Service.

Create   Cancel

3. On the right-hand side, you will see a tab named **Enabled APIs (7)**, as follows. Click on that tab:

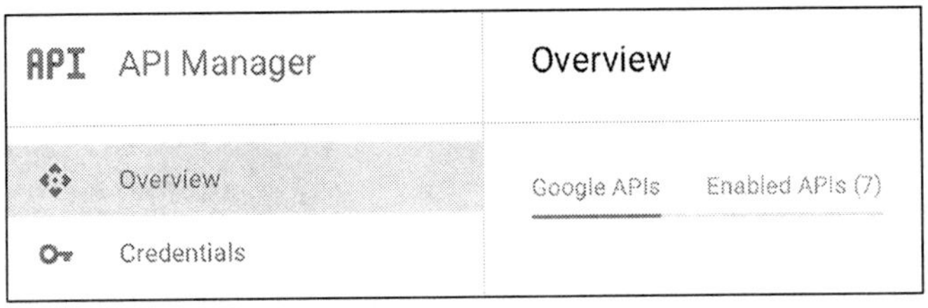

API API Manager | Overview

Overview

Credentials

Google APIs   Enabled APIs (7)

This will show you a list of APIs that are enabled by default. Since we will not use these APIs, click on the **Disable** option next to each API and disable each one of them.

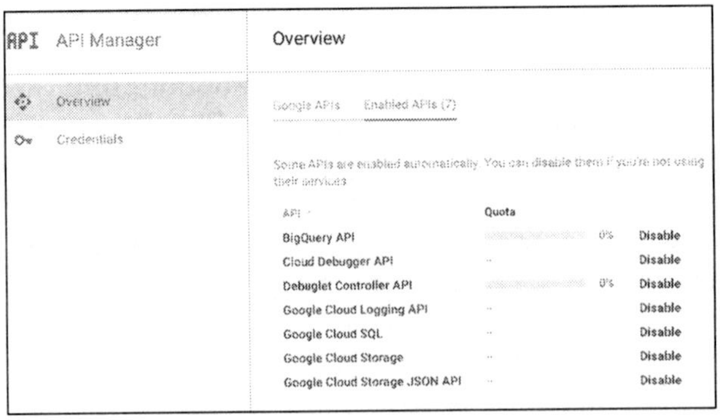

API API Manager | Overview

Overview

Credentials

Google APIs   Enabled APIs (7)

Some APIs are enabled automatically. You can disable them if you're not using their services

API	Quota		
BigQuery API		0%	Disable
Cloud Debugger API	--		Disable
Debuglet Controller API		0%	Disable
Google Cloud Logging API	--		Disable
Google Cloud SQL	--		Disable
Google Cloud Storage	--		Disable
Google Cloud Storage JSON API	--		Disable

After you have disabled all APIs, your screen will look like the following screenshot:

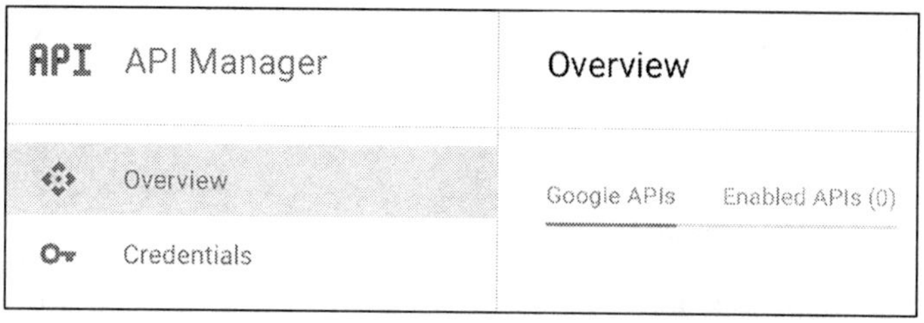

4. Our next goal is to enable the one API that our app will use—the **Fusion Tables API**. To do so, look for the **Other popular APIs** column. You will find it to the bottom-right group of links (look for the blue hexagon icon), as shown in the screenshot that follows:

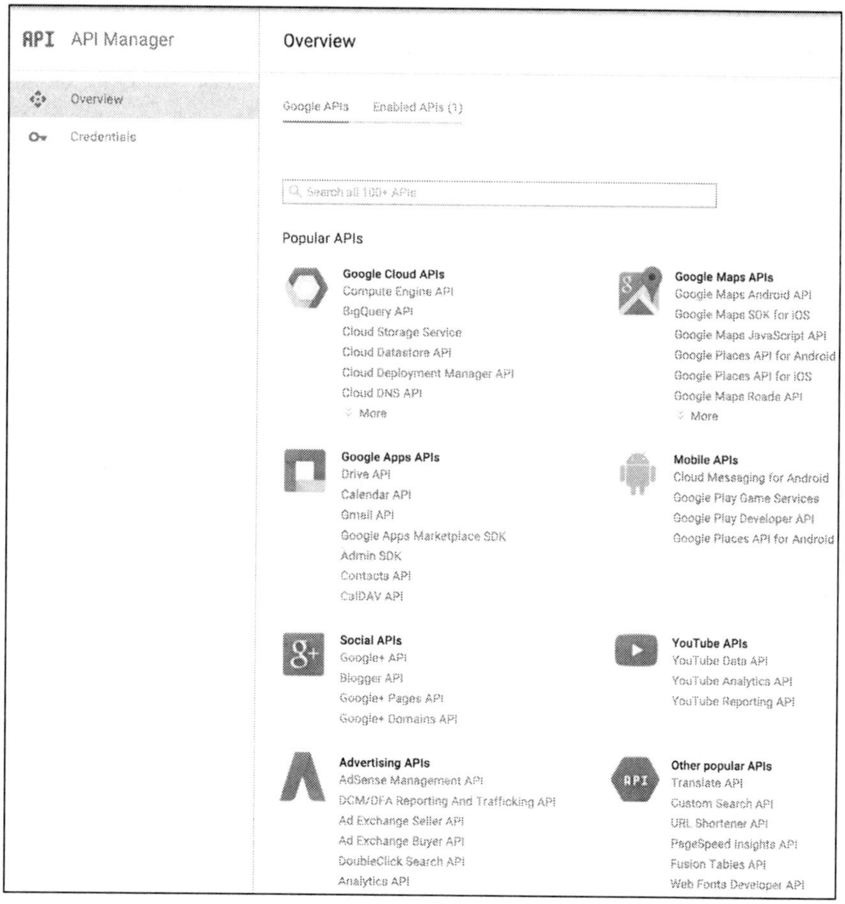

5. Click on the **Fusion Tables API** listed in this column. And then, in the next screen, click on the blue **Enable API** button shown in the following screenshot:

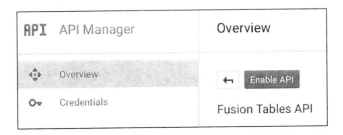

6. Now that we have enabled the **Fusion Tables API**, it is time to create credentials (ways for software to verify the authenticity of other software). Click on the **Credentials** option on the left vertical pane, as shown in the following screenshot:

This will result in a pop-up window with the blue **Add credentials** button, as shown in the following screenshot. Click on that button and select the last option—**Service account**.

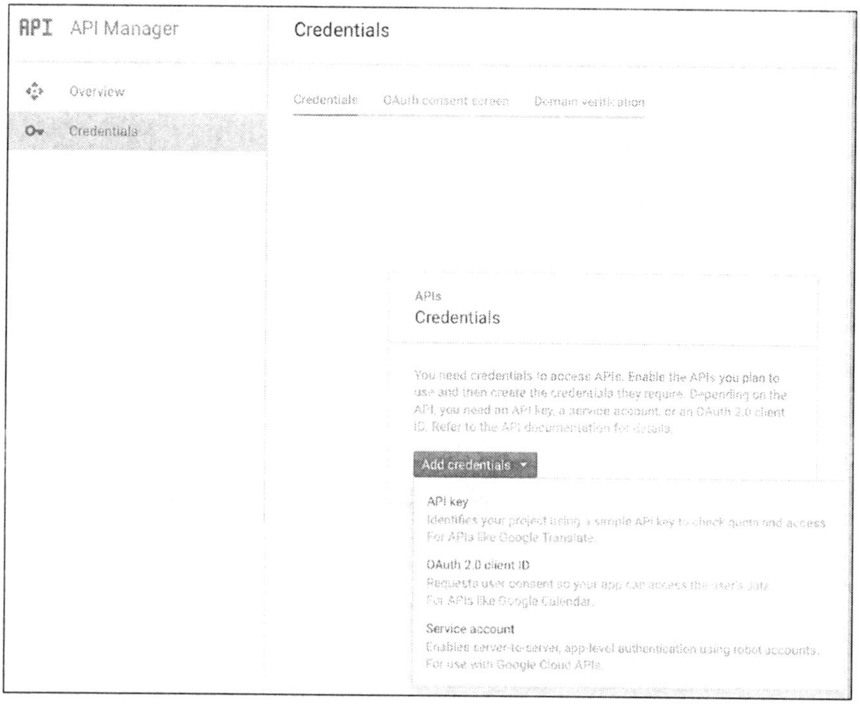

In the next window, make the selections shown in the following screenshot and click on **Create**:

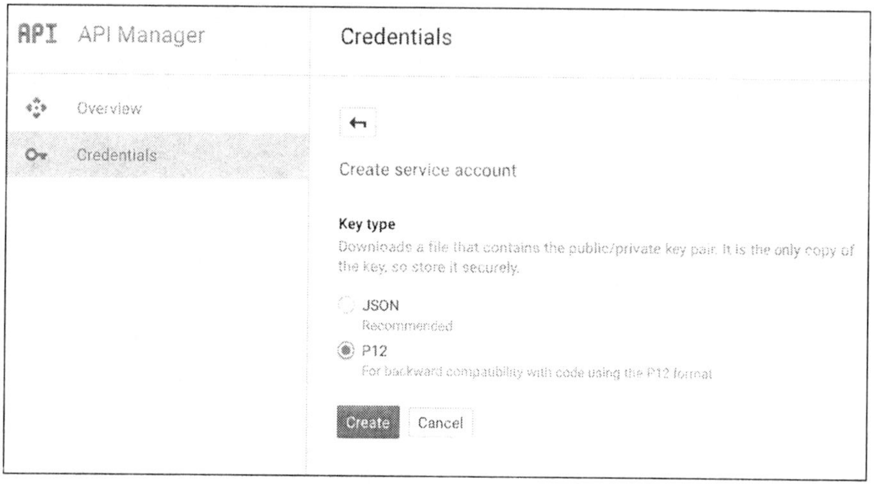

This will create the service account and download a special file onto your computer. This file has a `.p12` extension. Depending on your browser's setting, you might see a window such as the following one. This window asks you where to save the file. Save the file somewhere on your hard drive and remember the location. We will upload this file in to App Inventor later on:

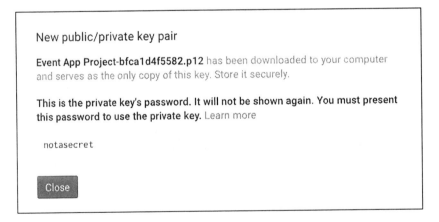

If you do not see the pop-up window like the one shown previously, in all likelihood your browser is set to download everything to the default `Downloads` folder. In that case, the `.p12` file will automatically be saved in that folder:

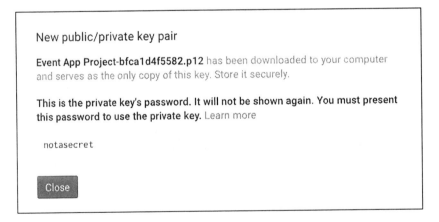

After this `.p12` file has been downloaded to to your computer, you will see a message resembling the one shown previously. Click the **Close** button to dismiss the message.

7. Now that we have created the credentials we are going to use, Google will automatically generate an e-mail address that goes with this credential. This email address is something we will have to specify in App Inventor as well. As shown in the following screenshot, a long and complicated email address will be displayed under the **Service** accounts. Copy this email and paste it into the document that you used to store the ID of the Fusion Table that you created earlier. Just like the ID of the Fusion Table, you will need this email address later on:

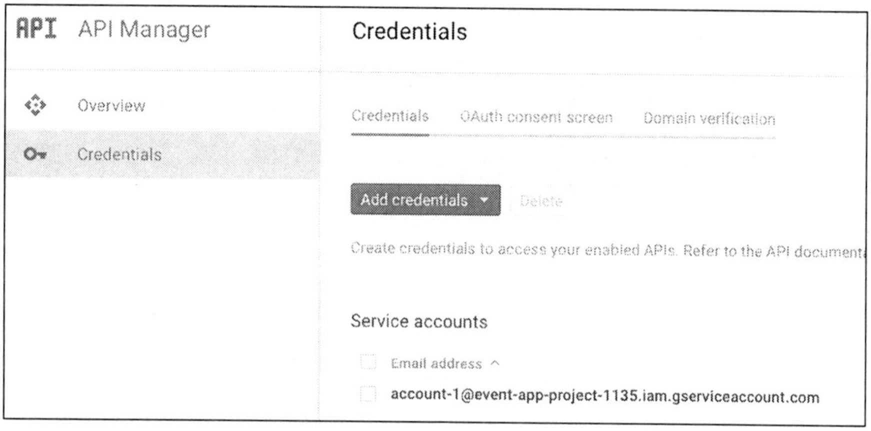

API API Manager	Credentials
⟡ Overview	Credentials OAuth consent screen Domain verification
⚲ Credentials	Add credentials ▾ Delete
	Create credentials to access your enabled APIs. Refer to the API document
	Service accounts
	☐ Email address ⌃
	☐ account-1@event-app-project-1135.iam.gserviceaccount.com

8. The **Fusion Tables API** is now enabled and the credentials are established.

Sharing the Fusion Table with the service account email

When you created the Fusion Table in a previous section, you used your own Google account to do so. So right now only you can access and change the Fusion Table. However, for this app to work, you need all your guests to have the ability to insert data into the Fusion Table and read from the Fusion Table.

The service account email that you created in the previous step will come in handy to achieve just that. That email is associated with your app and not any individual. Hence, anyone else using the app should be able to access the Fusion Table as long as that email address has proper access to the Fusion Table.

To enable the service level email access to the Fusion Table, go back to your Fusion Table (left open in the separate browser window/tab) and click on the blue **Share** button in the top-right corner. This will open the **Sharing settings** menu, as shown in the following screenshot.

Copy and paste the service email address that you saved earlier into the **Invite people** box. Make sure the button next to the box says **Can edit**, and click on **Send**.

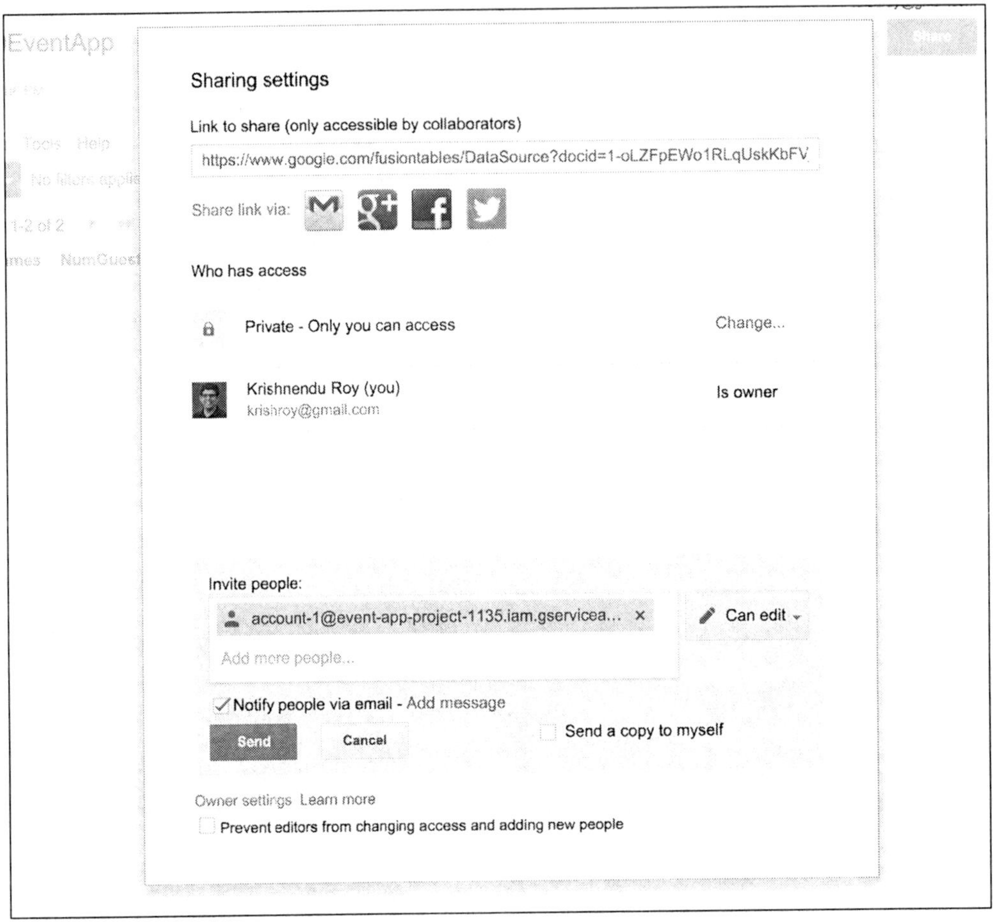

This step ensures that any user of the app (not just you) is able to insert data into or receive data from the Fusion Table.

Connecting the app to the Google Fusion Table

So far, we have created a Fusion Table and the GUI for the RSVP_Screen, and established our Google API credentials. Now it is time to create the code for RSVP_Screen.

Our goal

When the user clicks the **Send RSVP** button:

1. The app takes the name from the **NameTextBox**, the selection from the **NumGuestListPicker**, and the contents of the **ItemsBringingTextBox** and inserts them as a single row in the appropriate column in the Fusion Table.

2. Then the app clears textboxes and reset the Listpicker selection to 1.

We created the service-level credentials (the .p12 file and the service-level email address) so that our app is authorized to send or receive information from Google Fusion Tables. Next, we need to provide the **FusiontablesControl** component in our app with this information. We want to do this when a user opens the RSVP_Screen.

As shown in the following screenshot, once in the **RSVP_Screen** in the Designer, select the **FusionTablesControl1** component under the **Components** column. This will display all the properties of **FusiontablesControl1**. Under the **KeyFile** property, click currently shows **None**. Then click on the **Upload File** button:

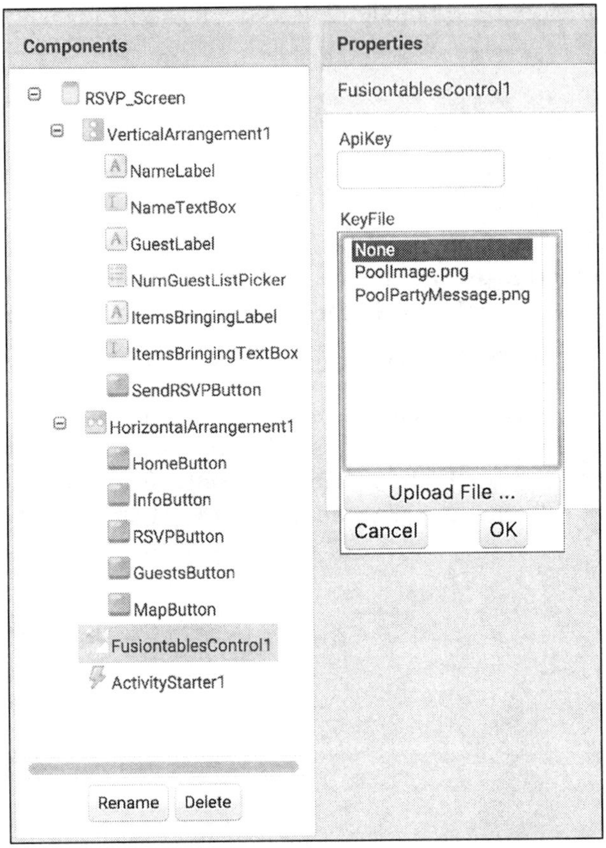

This will open up another pop-up, which will let you select the file that you want to upload. The following screenshot shows the pop-up. Select the `.p12` file that you earlier downloaded to your computer and click on the **OK** button:

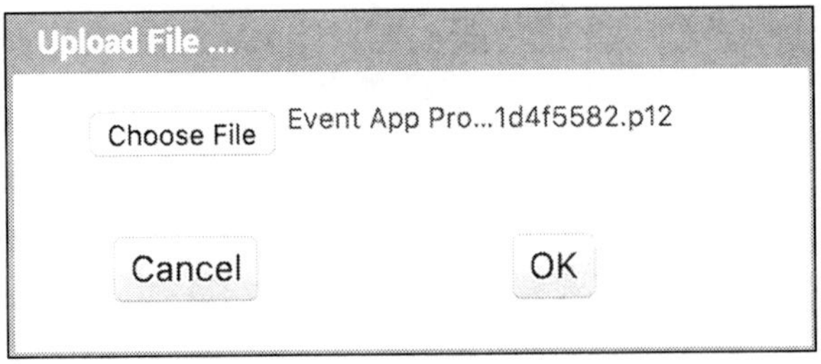

Next, copy the service-level email address that you have saved in a document and paste it into the **ServieAccountEmail** property.

Finally, check the **UserServiceAuthentication** checkbox.

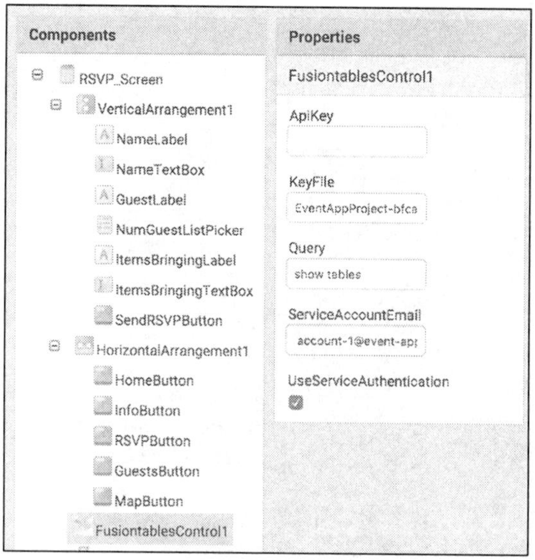

Pushing data to the Fusion Table

When using multiple screens, you want to keep your blocks organized according to screen in the Blocks editor. Since we are getting ready to program blocks for the RSVP_Screen, we need to make sure we are on the RSVP_Screen in the Blocks editor.

To check this, look at the first of three buttons in the green menu bar next to the EventApp name. If you just finished working on the RSVP_Screen in the Designer and switched over to the Blocks editor, you will be on RSVP_Screen. But if not, you can easily navigate to RSVP_Screen by clicking the button that displays another screen name (Screen1 as shown in the following screenshot) and choosing RSVP_Screen from the drop-down menu:

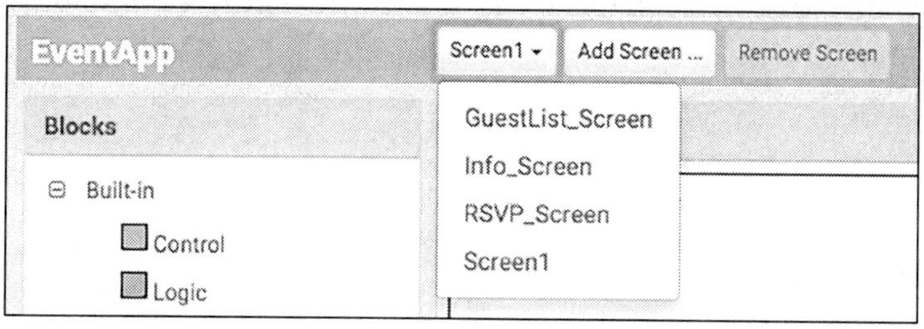

When the user clicks the **Send RSVP** button, we want to insert all three pieces of data into the Fusion Table. The following screenshot shows the block to achieve just this. This might look intimidating, but is actually quite simple:

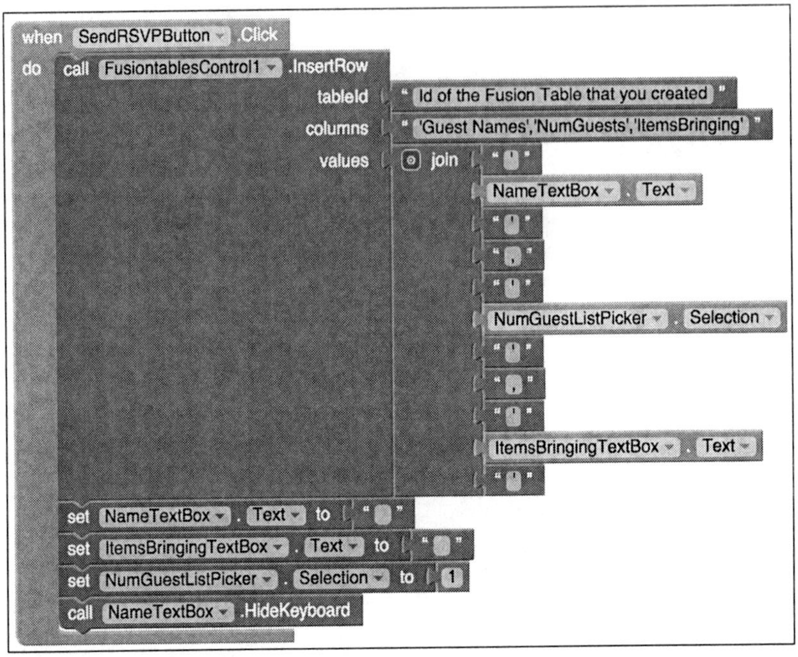

Since we want our app to react to the **Send RSVP** button click, we will of course need to get a **SendRSVPButton.Click** event. As you might have already guessed, you will find this event block in the Blocks Palette in the **SendRSVPButton** Blocks drawer.

The purple **call FusiontablesControl1.InsertRow** block enables an app to insert a row into a Fusion Table. In the **Fusiontables1** Blocks drawer, select and place the **FusiontablesControl1.InsertRow** block within the **SendRSVPButton.Click** event.

As you can see, the **InsertRow** block has three empty sockets. The first socket is the **Id** of the table that you want to use. Recall that we found the **Id** of our table during the last step when creating the table. Copy and paste that **Id** here within an empty **Text** block.

In the second socket of the **InsertRow** block, we will specify the column names. When inserting a row with multiple pieces (columns) of data into a Fusion Table, we need to specify which columns those pieces of data fit into. Recall that we named our columns **Guest Names**, **NumGuests**, and **ItemsBringing**. In a blank **Text** block, enter the column names within single-quotes, separated by commas, as shown in the following screenshot (note there are no spaces):

The third and final piece of information that the **InsertRow** block needs is the actual values to insert into the Fusion Table. Just like the column names, we will be entering multiple pieces of data into a single row in the Fusion Table. As with the columns, these three pieces of data must be entered within single quotes and separated by commas but we will insert them a little differently. To create one single-quoted, comma-separated text from three pieces of information that a guest will enters in the three separate fields in the **RSVP_Screen**, we will use a **join** block, From the built-in **Text** Block drawer, drag and connect the **join** block to the values socket of **InsertRow**.

We will need to join 11 things—three pieces of information, six single quotes (one before and one after each piece of information), and two commas to separate the three pieces of single-quoted information. By default, the **join** block joins two things. So we need to make room for nine more items. Click on the blue button on the top left corner of the **join** block, and drag the string block on the left of the pop-up into the join block on the right of the pop-up, shown as follows. This will create more sockets in the **join** block. Do this nine times:

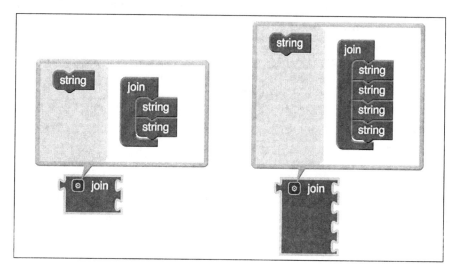

The first, third, fifth, seventh, ninth, and eleventh **join** sockets will contain a single quote, entered into a Text box. The fourth and eight sockets will contain a comma entered into a Text box. In the second socket, the app will get the first set of information that a user enters: their first and last name. So, we need a block that allows the user to enter a name. You will find it in the **NameTextBox** blocks. Select and connect the light green **NameTextBox.Text** block into the second join socket.

The sixth socket will get the number of guests that the user selected from the list picker. In the **NumGuestListPicker** blocks, select and connect the light-green **NumGuestListPicker.Selection** block. And in the tenth socket, the app will get the information about which food/drink item the user inputted. In the **ItemsBringingTextBox** blocks, select and connect the light green **ItemsBringingTextBox.Text** block.

Again, recall the first goal that we specified in this section: take the three pieces of information that a guest provides and insert them in the Fusion Table. The three pieces of data come from the **NameTextBox** text property, the **NumGuestListPicker** selection property, and the **ItemsBringingTextBox** text property. This step was a complicated one, but it is very important to get this set of blocks right because, if not, no data will be inserted into the Fusion Table.

Now that we are done with the **InsertRow** block, all that is left is to clear out the textboxes and revert the **ListPicker** selection to the default value of 1. Since blocks are executed from top to bottom and we want to clear out the Textboxes and reset the ListPicker after the app sends the information to the Fusion Table, insert the next set of blocks after the InsertRow block. Find the **set NameTextBox.Text to**, **set ItemsBringingTextBox.Text to**, and **set NumGuestListPicker.Selection** blocks and insert them into the bottom of the **when SendRSVPButton.Click** block. The first two blocks—**set NameTextBox.Text to** and **set ItemsBringingTextBox.Text to**—get blank Text blocks. Setting the textboxes to empty strings will clear out the previous data. Since we want the **set NumGuestListPicker.Selection** to reset the default selection property of the **NumGuestListPicker** to 1, attach a **Math 0** block and change the number to **1**. Lastly, we will call a procedure to make sure any keyboard that might have popped-up when the guest was typing in information gets hidden. Find the call **NameTextBox.HideKeyboard** block in the **NameTextBox** blocks. Connect it at the very bottom of the blocks.

Ensuring empty rows are not inserted

Right now, the **InsertRow** does not have any way to tell if the data that it is inserting is valid or not. For example, the user might click on the **SendRSVPButton** by mistake and that will insert a blank row. We can fix this by checking to make sure that the guest has typed in at least the name before we insert anything.

To achieve this, we can place all the blocks that we created within an if / then statement. The condition that we will check for is whether the NameTextBox. Text is empty or not. If the NameTextBox.Text is not empty, then that means the guest must have typed something and we will allow the insertion to happen. "If the NameTextBox.Text is empty, then the if statement is not true, and the then set of blocks will not fire. As a result, nothing will happen. The following screenshot shows the blocks for the if statement:

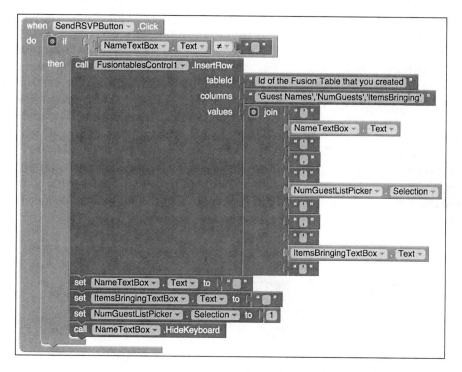

You can find the lime-green (unequal) block in the **Build In Logic** Block drawer. The block will appear with an equals sign, as follows:

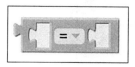

Click on the arrow and select the unequal option from the drop down menu. In the first blank, insert the **NameTextBox.Text** block and, in the second blank, insert a blank **Text** block. Now our code indicates that, if the name field is not blank, **then** it should get the data and insert it into the Fusion Table.

Viewing the guest list

Now that we have implemented the **RSVP_Screen**, we have a way for guests to send RSVPs and aggregate all the RSVPs from different guests into the Fusion Table. In any event organization app, it is helpful for others to be able to see a list of guests who have already RSVP'ed.

The purpose of the GuestList_Screen is just that—enabling all attendees (and the organizer) to see who else is coming to the event. To display information gathered in the Fusion Table, we will use a Label. In the Designer window, navigate to the **GuestList_Screen**. Just like in the RSVP_Screen, first drag a **VerticalArragment** to the top portion of the **GuestList_Screen**, above the **HorizontalArrangement**, which contains all the navigation buttons. Make the **BackgroundColor** property in **VerticalArrangement** to **None**. Also set both the **Height** and **Width** properties to **Fill parent**. Now drag a **Label** component into the **VerticalArrangement**. Rename the Label `GuestListLabel`. Change the **BackgroundColor** property of **GuestListLabel** to **None**. Change the **FontSize** property to **18** (you might have to try various values for this property depending on your device's screen size and screen resolution). Finally, change the **TextColor** property to **White**. Then add a **FusiontablesControl** component just like you did in the **RSVP_Screen**. You can view the changes in the following screenshot:

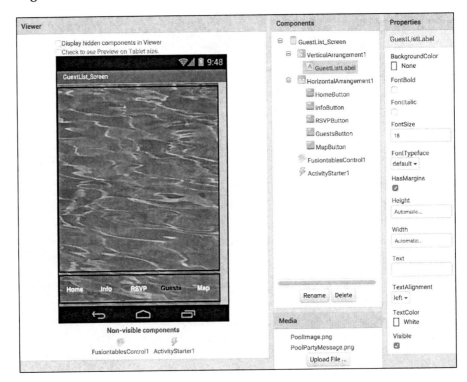

Just like in the **RSVP_Screen**. We will change the three properties of the **FusiontablesConrol1** component. Since you already know how to change the three **FusiontablesControl1** properties—**KeyFile**, **ServiceAccountEmail**, and **UseServiceAuthentication**—we will not go into the details here. Just follow the steps that we completed in the *Connecting the app to the Google Fusion Table* section.

Whereas in the RSVP_Screen, the app sends information to the Fusion Table, in the GuestList_Screen, the app is requests information from the Fusion Table, receives it and then displays it. To program this, head to the **Blocks** editor.

Coding the blocks – requesting data

The first code that we need to program is to request data from the Fusion Table. Click on **GuestList_Screen** in the Blocks drawer and drag the **when GuestList_Screen.Initialize** event. This event is automatically triggered whenever a screen is launched. We want to request data from the Fusion Table when the **GuestList** screen is launched. Thus, we will add to this event is the **call FusiontablesControl1.GetRows** block. This block will let us request data from the Fusion Table. You can find this block in the **FusiontablesControl1** blocks drawer. The **GetRows** block needs two pieces of information to fetch rows from Fusion Tables: the ID of the table and name of the column. We identified the table ID when we were creating the Fusion Table. Paste that ID into the **tableId** socket of the **GetRows** block using a **Text** block. Use another **Text** block to specify the column name, **'Guest Names'**. Note the single quotes; just like in the **InsertRows** block, the column names have to be single-quoted here as well. The following screenshot shows the completed set of blocks:

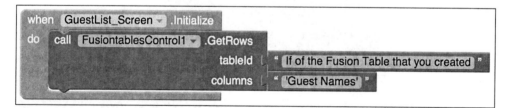

Coding the blocks – receiving data

The previous blocks request in data from the Fusion Table, now we need to code receiving the information from the Fusion Table. The **when FusiontablesControl1.GotResult** block does this. You will find it in the **FusiontablesControl1** blocks. As we mentioned before, when data from Fusion Tables is received, this event gets triggered. The data is placed in the **result** variable of this event.

By default, the data we receive from the Fusion Table is a block of text with each row placed on its own line. This data also includes the column header. So, let's say the Guest Names column of our Fusion Table has three rows with the names Olivienne, Dash, and Eva. Then the data that is placed in the result variable has four lines — Guest Names, Olivienne, Dash, and Eva (the column header followed by the three names).

Since we want the **when FusiontablesControl1.GotResult** event to automatically display the guest names (and the header), select and connect the **set GuestListLabel. Text to** block. What do we want it to display? The **result** variable. Hover your cursor over the light orange **result** variable embedded in the gold event block. A pop-up with two orange blocks will appear, as shown in the following screenshot. Select the **get result** block and attach it to the open socket in the **GuestListLabel.Text** block:

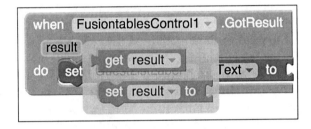

That's it! Now your **GuestList_Screen** will display all the guests who have RSVP'ed. The following screenshot shows the completed sets of blocks:

It is time to try your app! Fill out the RSVP form to see if it populates into your Fusion Table. Does the app then clear the RSVP screen fields and display the names in the **Guest List** screen?

If you recall, we set up our app to gather other data from the RSVP besides the list of guest names. We created fields so guests could input the number of people they are bringing and the food/drink item to share. You could also display this information for other guests to see, but really that data is for the host, who can easily view it along with the names in the Fusion Table columns we created.

Sharing the Event App

With the Event App, we wanted to introduce you to the process of collecting and retrieving data. Now that you are approaching apps from more of a developer's perspective, you will probably be aware that every time you enter your email address or other information into an app, that data is getting stored into a database. But, as we mentioned at the beginning of this chapter, Fusion Tables as a database has its limitations. If you were to share the Event App as it is with multiple event organizers, who start using it on different devices, there will be a problem because the app uses a single Fusion Table as the back end. If many people use the app for their different events, all of the data from all the different devices will be aggregated in to one single Fusion Table. Of course this will create mass confusion for the event organizers (and guests) as all of the data for different parties will be all mixed up!

Before we outline a possible fix to this problem, lets discuss what we did in this app. Since our app accesses and modifies the Fusion Table, we had to create Google service level authentication. This step ensures that our app is authorized by Google to access Fusion Tables. Then, we inserted the Fusion Table Id into our app to let the app know which Fusion Table to access. Additionally, we created a service email address for our app and shared the Fusion Table with this service email address. These steps ensure that the Fusion Table allows our app to read/write data. So we basically had three different entities interacting with each other - Google service level authentication, our app, and the Fusion Table.

One way to address the problem of the single Fusion Table associated with the Event App is for the developer to create different copies of the app that uses different copies of a Fusion Table. This means that each copy of the app will have to be updated with the Id of the new copy of the Fusion Table. Additionally, this also means the Fusion Table will have to be re-shared with the app's service level email (using the original service email address).

It is easier than it sounds. First, open the Fusion Table that you used previously, go to the File menu and select, Make a copy. This will create a new copy of the original Fusion Table with all of the changes we made to the columns and settings. If your previous Fusion Table had any data in it, you will need to clear the data. Next, repeat the Fusion Table Id identification step outlined in the last few paragraphs of Creating a Google Fusion Table section. (Since you are creating a new Fusion Table, you will have to use the Id of this new table.) You will also have to repeat the Sharing the Fusion Table with the service account email section for this new Fusion Table (using the original service email address).

Lastly, in Blocks editor, paste the new Fusion Table Id into the Text box (attached to the TableID slot of the call FusiontablesControl1.InsertRow block) to ensure that the app uses the new Fusion Table.

 If you want to share your Event App with 7 people, you will need to repeat these steps 7 times, so that each person has a unique version of the app with a unique Fusion Table.

Summary

In this chapter we explored a lot of App Inventor advanced features, namely a database. Google Fusion Tables makes it possible for us to store data in the backend. We learned how to create a new Fusion Table and how to establish Google API credentials so that our app is authorized to access Google Fusion Tables. Finally we learned how to insert, retrieve, and display data from the Fusion Tables.

You are amassing quite a programming toolkit! And in the next chapter, you will learn yet another tool to help expand your coding skills. A loop is a structure or sequence of instructions that enables you to iterate or repeat steps until certain conditions are met. This is handy because, instead of copying and pasting blocks to perform the same function for each item in a long list, we can program one set of blocks to execute repeatedly.

7
Learning About Loops with a Raffle App

In the previous chapters, you used the `if-then-else` control block several times. The **if then else** block enables apps to make decisions. It is one of the fundamental computing concepts that is present in any programming language. There is a second fundamental programming concept—the **loop**, which we will explore in this chapter. A loop allows a program to repeat code. More specifically, in App Inventor, a loop will let us execute a stack of blocks multiple times.

To illustrate the concept of a loop, we will create a digital raffle App in this chapter. In case you aren't familiar with a regular (nondigital) raffle, we will explain. A raffle organizer gives participants a ticket with a number on it and puts a duplicate of that ticket in a bowl. When all the tickets have been given out (and put in the bowl), the raffle organizer then randomly picks a ticket out of the bowl (often times with a blindfold on) and announces the winning ticket number. The participant with the matching ticket number then claims a prize.

Creating a digital raffle app using App Inventor is not a new idea. Others have created similar apps before. For example, `http://www.appinventor.org/content/howDoYou/RecordingInfo/phone` shows how to create a very simple digital raffle app. We will extend this idea and create a more versatile digital raffle app. For our digital Raffle App, participants send a text message with a specific code to the raffle organizer. The raffle organizer runs the app on his or her phone, which keeps track of all the participants' incoming text messages and phone numbers and selects a random winner. Then, the app notifies the winner that she or he has won and notifies the rest of the participants that they did not win. This is a fun participatory game for a party, event, or a meeting break.

In this chapter, you will learn how to do the following:

- Create a user interface for the Raffle App
- Create and initialize a list and a variable
- Use a texting component to send/receive text messages
- Add items to a list
- Select a random winner
- Notify the winner that he or she has won
- Use a loop to send the same notification e-mail to all the participants who did not win
- Clear out the list and the variable

Creating the project and building the GUI

In preparation of using the Raffle App, the raffle organizer will give two pieces of information to everyone who wishes to participate in the raffle: the organizer's phone number and a code. The raffle organizer can distribute this information by either sharing them verbally or writing then down for everyone to see. The participants will then send a text message to the raffle organizer's phone number with the code typed in the body of the text message. When the app (running on the raffle organizer's phone) receives all of the text messages containing the code, it will save the all the senders' phone numbers in a list. Then, the raffle organizer will click on a button to randomly select a winner from the list of phone numbers. The winning phone number will be displayed on the raffle organizer's phone screen, and the app will also send a text message notification to the winner's phone indicating that he or she has won. Meanwhile, the app will notify the rest of the participants that they did not win.

Creating a new project

You will start by creating a new project. At this point, this step will probably be very familiar to you as you have already done this several times in the previous chapters. As shown in the following screenshot, click on the **Start new project** button after logging into App Inventor. Then, in the following pop-up message box, give an appropriate name for this app. We will use the name Digital_Raffle.

Creating the User Interface (UI)

Now that we have created a new project, it is time to add the first component that we will use, a Label. The raffle organizer will create a code to share with all the participants. Since the raffle organizer may conduct several raffles, we will use a label to display the code on the organizer's phone. For this app, we chose the code: **I want to win**. We will program the app to compare this code, **I want to win**, to any text message that the raffle organizer's phone receives. If it is a match, the app will save the associated phone number into a list. As shown in the following screenshot, drag a **Label** from the **User Interface** Palette drawer onto the **Viewer**:

At this time, we would like to reiterate the importance of naming components appropriately. Proper naming helps programmers when they are creating behavior in the Blocks editor. Additionally, appropriate names make it easier to understand the logic of the code. Lastly, should you decide to extend this app six months after first creating it, aptly named components will help you remember the purpose of each component.

Given that, rename **Label1** as `CodeLabel`. To rename **Label1**, select **Label1** in the **Components** column. Recall that selecting a component will make its background green on the screen, which indicates that it is active. Then, click on the **Rename** button at the bottom of the panel. In the pop-up window, enter the new name.

We will use this label to display the code (text) **I want to win**. Enter **I want to win** (without the quotes) in the **Text** property box. To make the code easily visible, we make the **FontSize** property 45. Finally, set **Width** of this label to **Fill parent**.

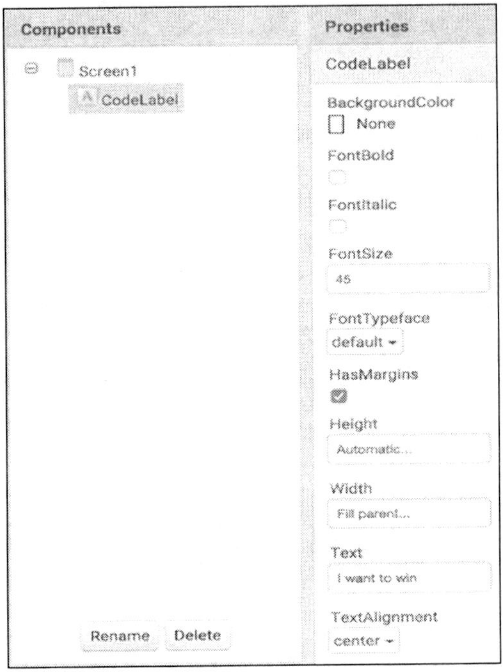

Next, we will add a button right below **CodeLabel**. This is the button that the raffle organizer will click on to select a winner. Drag a **Button** from the **User Interface** palette onto the **Viewer**, as shown in the following screenshot:

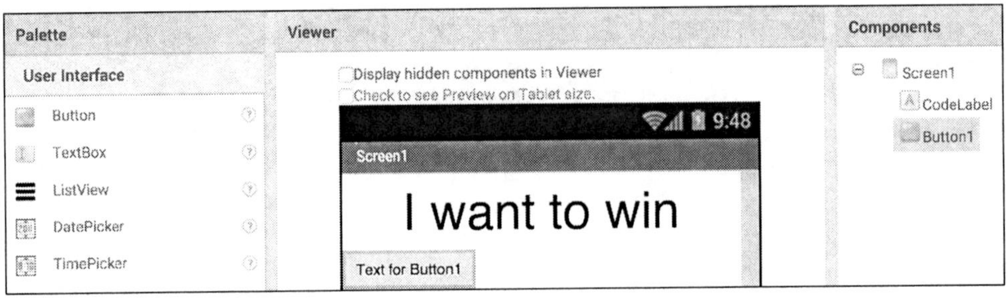

Rename **Button1** to `WinnerButton`. By default, the **Text** property of the button shows **Text for Button1**. Change the **Text** property to something more informative by clicking in the text box and typing **Pick Winner**. Also, change the **Width** property to **Fill parent** so that the button is of the same width as the label above it.

After adding CodeLabel and WinnerButton, add a third component, another label, to display the phone number of the winner. Just like the **CodeLabel**, Drag another **Label** below WinnerButton and rename it, `WinnerLabel`. Since we will only use this label after a winner is selected, thus delete everything under the **Text** property, so that **WinnerLabel** does not show anything. To have a consistent look, set the **Width** property to **Fill parent**.

Finally, set the **FontSize** property to 35 so that the winner's phone number when displayed is not too small. The following screenshot shows the app after **WinnerLabel** is added and configured:

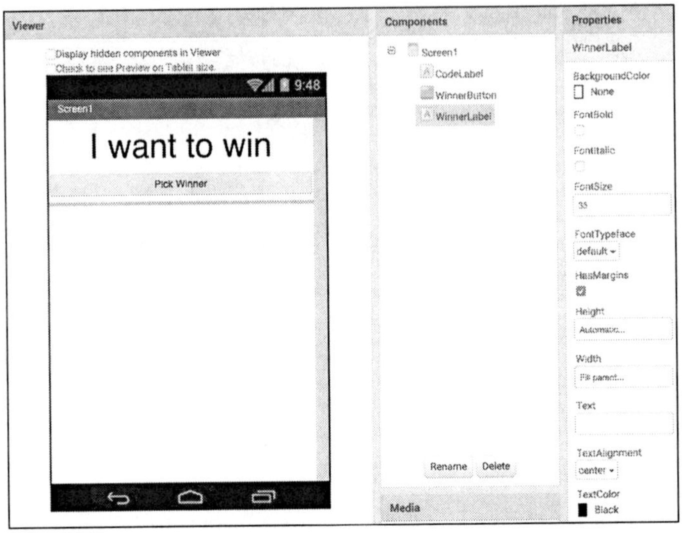

Since the Raffle app might be used many times, we need to have a mechanism to reset the app. For this purpose, add one more button below **WinnerLabel**. Rename it `ClearButton`, change the **Width** property of the button to **Fill parent**, and finally, change the **Text** property to `Clear`, as shown in the following screenshot:

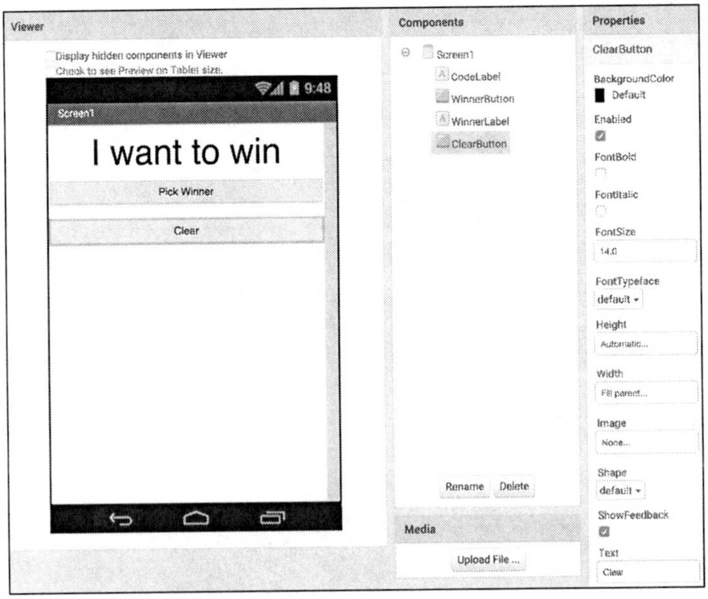

Next, we need some way for the app to send and receive text messages. For this, use the **Texting** component. You will find the **Texting** component in the **Social** Palette drawer. Drag the **Texting** Component onto the **Viewer**. As shown in the following image, the **Texting** component is a **Non-visible component** and is housed below the Viewer. We do not need to set any properties for this component.

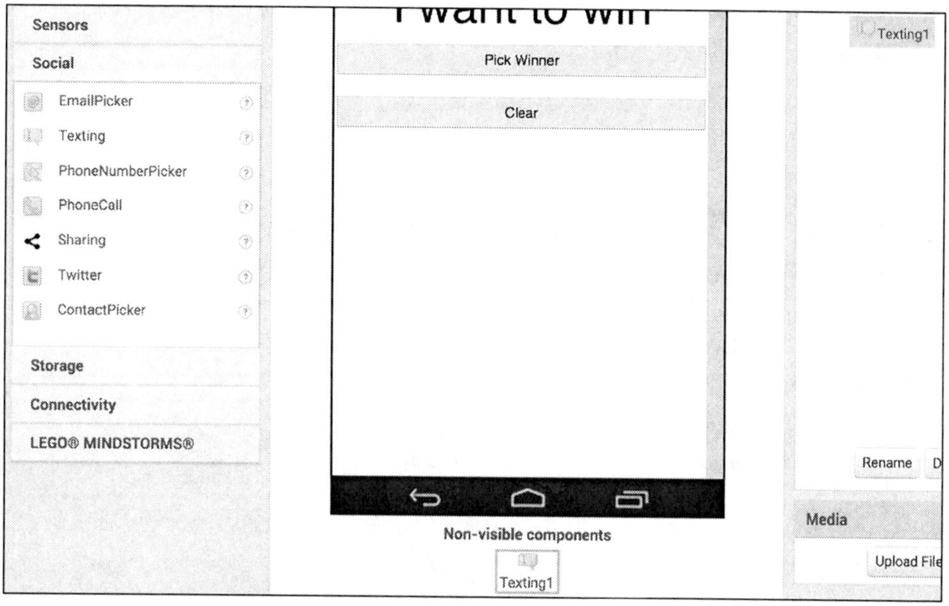

This completes the GUI of the Raffle app. In the next section, we will program the behavior of the app in Blocks editor.

Programming the behavior of the Digital Raffle app

To summarize, when the app receives text messages from participants, if a text message contains the indicated code (in this case, **I want to win**) in the body of the message, then the sender's phone number is added to a list. When the raffle organizer clicks the WinnerButton, the app will randomly select a winner from that list of phone numbers. Then, the app will send the winner a text message notifying him or her of the win. The app will also send text messages to all the other participants letting them know that they did not win.

We will achieve all of this by completing the following substeps:

- Create and initialize a list and a variable
- Receive text messages, and if the code matches, add the sender's number to the list
- Select a random item from the list (winner)
- Send a winner notification
- Send other participants a notification letting them know that they did not win

Creating and initializing the variable and list

For this app, we will need a list to store all the participant's phone numbers. And we will also use a variable to temporarily store the winning number. To create the list and the variable, go to the **Variables** blocks panel and drag the topmost block **initialize global name** to as shown in the following screenshot. Do this twice.

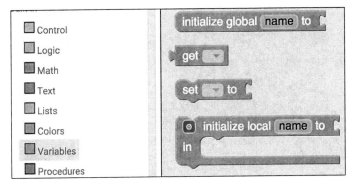

Double-click on "**name**" inside both the blocks and type in new names, **ListOfNumbers** for the list and **WinningNumber** for the variable, as shown in the following screenshot:

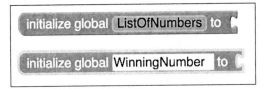

Whenever you (as a programmer) create a list or variable, you need to initialize it with an initial value. For our list, we want to start out with an empty list. App Inventor makes this easy. In the **Lists** blocks, select the **create empty list** block, as shown in the following screenshot, and connect it to the **initialize global ListOfNumbers to** block:

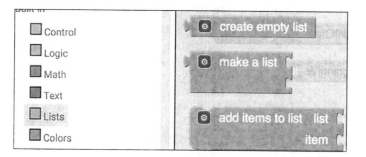

For the **WinningNumber** variable, we will initialize it to be 0. In the **Math** blocks, select the **0** block (shown in the following screenshot) and connect it to the **initialize global WinningNumber to** block:

After completing these steps, the initialization blocks for the list and the variable will look like the following screenshot:

Receiving text messages from participants

In this section, you will learn how to receive text messages from participants and store their numbers in a list.

We added the nonvisible Texting1 component in the Designer tab when we created the UI. We will use this component to send and receive text messages. As shown in the following screenshot, this component has a single gold event block, when Texting1.MessageReceived. Whenever the raffle organizer's device receives any text message, this event will get triggered.

Click on the **when Texting1.MessageReceived** event block to add it to the **Viewer**. As shown in the following screenshot, this event has two associated variables—**number** and **messageText**. Whenever a text message is received and this event is triggered, the **number** variable contains the sender's phone number and **messageText** contains the content of the message.

> When you want to store some data, you can create global variables. In previous steps, we explicitly created our own global variables called **ListOfNumbers** and **WinningNumber** and initialized them. Once you create a global variable, any block in your app can use that variable.
>
> On the other hand, when an app is running, various events might also need to temporarily store data and hence, may need a variable. These variables, which are built into blocks, are called local variables. They appear in a block and can be accessed by hovering over them with a mouse. Their existence is limited to a particular event. Other blocks of the app cannot use them. In fact, if you try to use a variable outside the event block that they are a part of, you will get an error message. Examples of local variables are **number** and **messageText**; they are associated specifically with the block, **when Texting1.MessageReceived**.

Thus, the **number** and **messageText** variables store important data related to the **when Texting1.MessageReceived** event block. Whenever a text message is received, this event is triggered and the information related to the text message (the sender's number and the message text) is placed into these two variables and can be used by the blocks within that event.

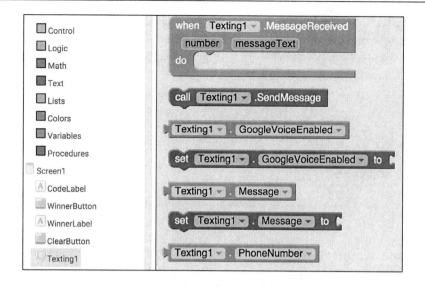

Since the raffle organizer's phone can receive text messages unrelated to the raffle at the same time that it receives raffle text messages, we want to filter out the raffle related text messages. This is the main reason we include the code (**I want to win**) in our design, to filter out raffle related text messages.

Recall that the **messageText** variable associated with the **when Texting1. MessageReceived** event contains the text of the message. So, once a text message is received, we want the app to check whether the **messageText** variable matches **I want to win** or not. Can you think of what type of block we would use to determine whether or not the code matches?

If you thought of an **if then** block, you are right! Do you recall where to find it? Select an **if then** block and connect it to the **when Texting1.MessageReceived** event. As you already know, we need to plug in a condition block into the if socket. In this case, we want to match two texts. App Inventor makes this easy. As shown in the following screenshot, in the **Text** blocks, select and connect the **compare texts** block to the empty **if** socket:

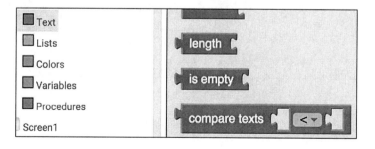

Since we want to check whether the two texts match, click on the downward pointing triangle next to the less-than sign and select the equals sign, as shown in the following screenshot:

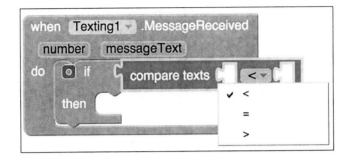

Hover the mouse pointer over the light orange **messageText** variable in the event block. This will trigger a pop-up window, as shown in the following screenshot. Select the **getMessageText** block and place it within the first opening in the **compare texts** block to the left of the equals sign. This block will get the text from the incoming text message (any text message):

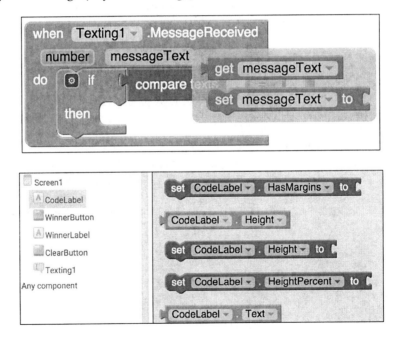

For the second opening, we want to input the code we created so we can compare it to the text message received. If you recall, in the `Designer` property, we set the `Text` property of **Codelabel** to our code, **I want to win**. So, under **Screen1**, go to the **CodeLabel** blocks and select the **CodeLabel.Text** block.

Insert the **CodeLabel.Text** block into the opening to the right of the equals sign in the **compare texts** block, as shown in the following screenshot. We have now programmed the app to check to see whether the text message (**messageText**) matches the `Text` property of the **CodeLabel** (the code, **I want to win**).

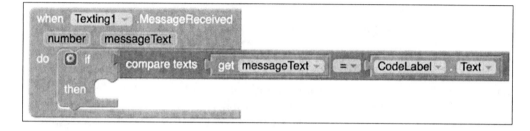

Adding the phone numbers of all the participants to the list

If the text message indeed contains the correct code, we know that the text message came from a raffle participant. Thus, we want the app to add the sender's phone number to the list that we created earlier. To do this, go to the **List** blocks and select the **add items to list** block, as shown in the following screenshot. Add it to the **then** opening of the **if/then** block.

The **add items to list** block needs two pieces of information, which we will attach to the empty sockets — the name of the list to add items to and the item to be added. To specify the list, go to the **Variables** block and select the **get** block and connect it to the **list** socket of the **add items to list** block.

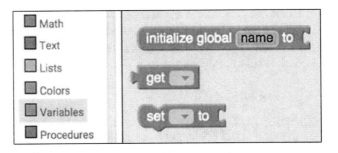

Then, click on the downward pointing triangle of the **get** block and select **global ListOfNumbers** from the drop-down menu as shown in the following screenshot. When we initialize a global variable, like we did for **ListOfNumbers**, it is then available for us to use throughout the app. This is why the name appears in the drop-down menu as an option.

As we mentioned before, the **number** variable associated with this **Texting1. MessageReceived** block contains the sender's phone number. You can use the **get number** block to access this number. Hover your mouse over **number** variable to view the pop-up window, as shown in the following image. Select the **get number** block and connect it to the **item** socket of the **add items to list** block.

The following screenshot shows the completed set of blocks for receiving text messages:

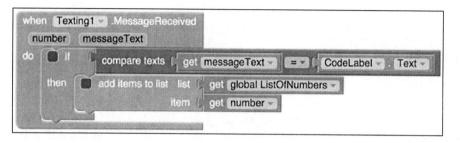

Thus far, we have programmed the app to do the following: receive text messages, verify that the message texts contains the **I want to win** code, and if so, add the sender's phone number to the list that we created (**ListOfNumbers**). If the text message does not match the CodeLabel Text, then nothing happens (the phone number does not get added to the list.)

Selecting a winner

When designing the UI, we added a **WinnerButton** that the raffle organizer will click to randomly select a winner. App Inventor also makes this easy. We will use the **pick a random item** block to select a winner from **ListOfNumbers**. You can find the **pick a random item** block under the **Lists** Blocks, as shown in the following screenshot:

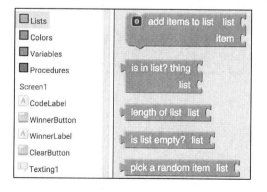

Since the raffle organizer will click a button to pick a winner select the **WinnerButton.Click** event (found in the **WinnerButton** blocks). Next, go to the **Variables** blocks, select a **set to** block, and place it within the **WinnerButton.Click** event. In the **set to** block, click on the downward pointing triangle and select **global WinningNumber**. Connect to this block with the **pick a random item** block that we selected earlier. The **pick a random item** block has an open socket indicating a list. Can you figure out which block would connect to it? Since we want the random item (phone number) to be selected from our list of numbers, copy and paste the **get global ListOfNumbers** block from the **add items to list** block (in the previous section) and connect it to the **pick a random item** block. The following screenshot shows the completed set of blocks up to this point:

What exactly are we coding here? We are programming the app to select a random item (phone number) from the list (of all the phone numbers) and store it in the **WinningNumber** variable (**set global WinningNumber to block**). You might be wondering why do we need to do this. As it will be evident later in this chapter, we will reuse this winning number several times. Hence, we need to temporarily store it somewhere.

Once we get the winning number, we want the app to display the winning number on the organizer's phone. To do this, we will set the **Text** property of **WinnerLabel** to **WinningNumber**. As shown in the following screenshot, select **set WinnerLabel. Text to** (under the **WinnerLabel** blocks) and connect it to the **get global WinningNumber** block (which you will find in the **Variables** block drawer). It will be listed just as an orange **get** block, and you will need to click on the downward pointing triangle to select **global WinningNumber** from the drop-down list. Your blocks should resemble those in the following screenshot:

Let's recap. We have programmed the app to randomly select a winner (phone number) from all the participant phone numbers (global **ListOfNumbers**), we will have saved the winning phone number into the **Variable Global WinningNumber** variable and displayed the winning number in **WinnerLabel**. The next step is notifying the winner by sending a text message to the winning number.

Notifying the winner

The non-visible **Texting1** component that we used before to receive the text messages from participants will be used here again. To send a text message to the winner, we will set both the **Texting1.Message** property and the **Texting1.PhoneNumber** property. Find the set blocks under the **Texting1** blocks. Select and place them inside the **WinnerButton.Click** event, as shown in the following screenshot. For the **Texting1.Message** property, connect a **blank Text** block and type in the message "**Congratulations!! You won**". For the **Texting1.PhoneNumber** property, copy and paste the **global WinningNumber** block and connect it to the empty socket.

The **Texting1** component has a purple block called **call Texting1.SendMessage**. This is the block that actually sends a text message. The **PhoneNumber** property of the **Texting1** component is used for the recipient's number and the **Message** property is used for the body of the text. Hence, it is important to set these two properties correctly before actually sending the text with the **call Texting1. SendMessage** block. As shown in the following screenshot, go to the **Texting1** blocks again, and drag the purple **call Texting1.SendMessage** block and place it at the bottom of all the blocks:

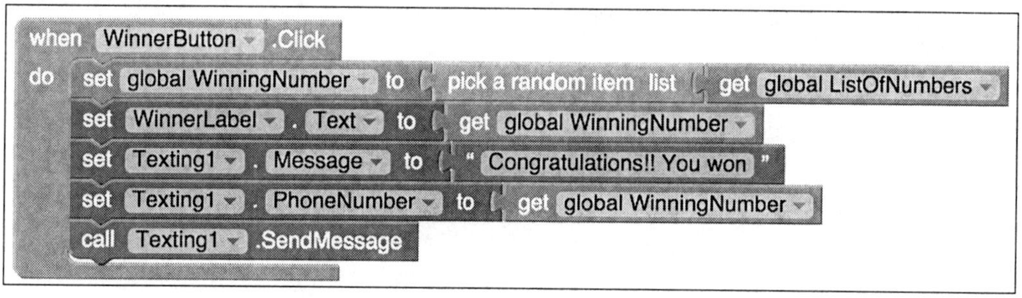

```
when  WinnerButton  .Click
do    set  global WinningNumber  to    pick a random item  list    get  global ListOfNumbers
      set  WinnerLabel  .  Text  to    get  global WinningNumber
      set  Texting1  .  Message  to    "  Congratulations!! You won  "
      set  Texting1  .  PhoneNumber  to    get  global WinningNumber
      call  Texting1  .SendMessage
```

We have now coded the Raffle app to send a congratulatory notification to the winner.

Notifying everyone else

Usually, the winner is excited to have won, and announces aloud that she or he has won. But in case this doesn't happen, we want to send a notification message to all the participants who did not win to ensure that no one is left wondering about the raffle outcome. It seems logical to send a **"Sorry, You did not win"** notification to all the items in **ListOfNumbers**, since it is storing all of the participants' phone numbers. However, there is a flaw to this logic. Can you guess what the problem is? Currently, **ListOfNumbers** contains all of numbers, including the winning number. So, before we use the **ListOfNumbers** as the source for the "**Sorry**" notification, we need to remove the winning number from this list.

As shown in the following screenshot, we will use the **remove list item** block to remove the winning number. You can find **remove list item** in the **List** blocks. This block needs two pieces of information (hence, the two empty sockets): the name of the list and the position (index) of the item to be removed. Specifying the name of the list is easy. Just copy and paste and connect the **global ListOfNumbers** block.

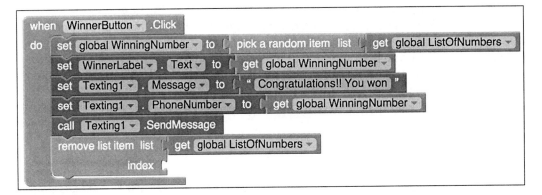

Finding the position of the winning number is a little more involved. We will need to add another **List** block, that is, the **index in list** block to figure out this position. As shown in the following screenshot, connect the **index in list** block to the empty **index** socket in the **remove list item** block:

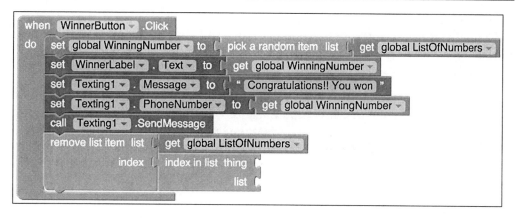

> **Index** is the position of an item in a list.
>
> The **remove** list item block can remove an item from a certain position. First, we need to figure out the position of the winning number (the thing) in the list. Then, we will use this position to remove the winning number.

The **index in list** block finds the position of the item specified in the **thing** socket from the list specified in the **list** socket. So, we will copy and paste, connect the get **global WinningNumber** block to the **thing** socket, and add another **get global ListOfNumbers** block to the **list** socket. Your code will look as follows:

```
when  WinnerButton  .Click
do    set global WinningNumber  to   pick a random item  list   get global ListOfNumbers
      set  WinnerLabel  .  Text  to   get global WinningNumber
      set  Texting1  .  Message  to   " Congratulations!! You won "
      set  Texting1  .  PhoneNumber  to   get global WinningNumber
      call  Texting1  .SendMessage
      remove list item  list   get global ListOfNumbers
                 index   index in list  thing   get global WinningNumber
                                         list   get global ListOfNumbers
```

Let's recap. We have identified the position of the winning number in the list and have removed the item at that position, thereby removing the winning number from the list. Now, we are ready to use this list to send a notification to the participants who did not win.

Just like the notification message we created for the winner previously, we will reuse the **Texting1** component to send out notifications to all the participants who did not win. Copy and paste the **set Texting1. Message to** block (that will copy the attached text block). Change the text in the Text block from "**Congratulations !! You won**" to "**Sorry, You did not win**". Feel free to change this message and personalize it to your liking.

Note that blocks execution is always top down. So effectively, the winning number is removed from **ListOfNumbers** before the notification is sent to the losing participants. And, **Texting1.Message** set to the block message "**Sorry, You did not win.**" overwrites the previous text message "**Congratulations!! You won**".

```
when  WinnerButton  .Click
do   set  global WinningNumber  to    pick a random item  list    get  global ListOfNumbers
     set  WinnerLabel . Text  to    get  global WinningNumber
     set  Texting1 . Message  to    " Congratulations!! You won "
     set  Texting1 . PhoneNumber  to    get  global WinningNumber
     call  Texting1 .SendMessage
     remove list item  list    get  global ListOfNumbers
                       index    index in list  thing    get  global WinningNumber
                                        list    get  global ListOfNumbers
     set  Texting1 . Message  to    " Sorry, You did not win "
```

An important difference between sending the notification to the winner and this notification is that this notification will be sent to *all* the numbers in the list **ListOfNumbers**, except the winning number. Essentially, this means that we need to repeat the **set Texting1.PhoneNumber to** block, followed by the **callTexting1. SendMessage** block—once for each item in **ListOfNumbers**. And this brings us to the concept of loops!

Using loops

A basic programming concept present in any programming language, including App Inventor, is called loop. Loops let us repeat code and thus we will use a loop here. We will place two blocks in the loop: **set Texting1.PhoneNumber to** and **call Texting1.SendMessage**.

Loops are available in the **Control** blocks drawer. There are different types of loops. We will use the **for each item in list** loop, as shown in the following screenshot. Select the **for each item in list** loop and place it at the bottom of the **when WinnerButton.Click** event. This loop requires us to specify a list that will be used in conjunction with the loop. The loop lets us repeat whatever block we place within the loop once for each item in the associated list. While the loop is running, during any iteration, the corresponding item from the list will be placed in the item variable as well. When the loop executes for the first time, the first item of **ListOfNumbers** will be available in the item variable associated with the loop. Similarly, when the loop executes for the second time, the second item will be available in the item variable and so on:

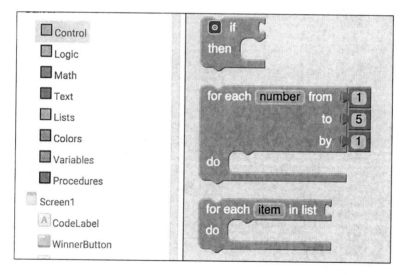

This loop will execute as many times as the number of number of phone numbers in **ListOfNumbers**. To specify the list, just copy and paste and connect the **get global ListOfNumbers** block to the empty list socket in the loop.

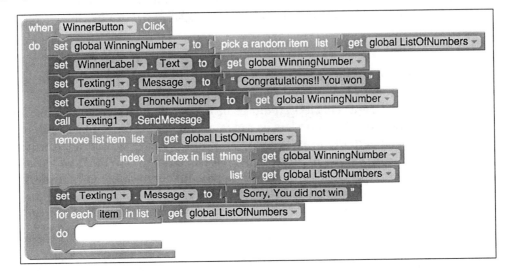

Now that the outline of the loop is ready, we need specify the body of the loop. First, drag the **set Texting1.PhoneNumber to** block into the *do* part of the loop, as shown in the following screenshot:

Next, hover your mouse over the item variable in the **for each item in list** block, and drag the **get item** block and connect it to the empty socket in the **set Texting1. PhoneNumber to** block, as shown in the following screenshot:

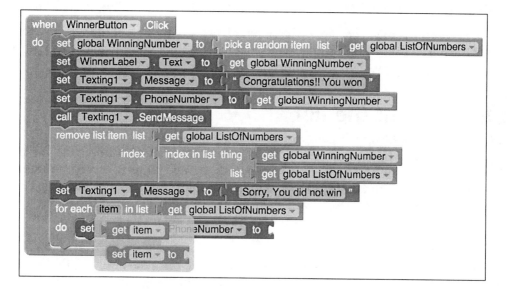

Next, copy and paste and place the purple **call Texting1.SendMessage** block into the **do** part of the loop at the very bottom, as shown in the following screenshot:

This loop accesses each item on the list one at a time, sets it as **Texting1. PhoneNumbers**, and sends out a text message to that phone number. So, this loop is allowing us to repeat the **set Texting1.PhoneNumber to** block, followed by the **call Texting1.SendMessage** block multiple times (for each item in **ListofNumbers**).

The digital raffle is now complete. The winner has been notified of the win and the rest of the participants have been notified that they did not win (note that a prize of some sort is usually given to the winner).

Clearing out the list and variable

After using the Raffle app, if you want to conduct another raffle with a different group of participants, you will need to clear out the list **ListOfNumbers** the variable **WinningNumber**, two things that were expressly created by us (the programmers). The other variables used in the app were local variables (**number** and **messageText** from the **Texting1.MessageReceived** event). These were not created by us, but rather generated by the blocks themselves; thus, these are used and cleared out automatically by the program.

There are two ways to clear out the list and variable to reset the app. The first way doesn't require programming. You can simply close the application and reopen it. This will reset the list to empty and the **WinningNumber** to 0. Can you guess the second way to reset the app? If you recall, we created a **ClearButton** feature for the UI in the Designer. We can program this **ClearButton** to clear out the app.

In the **ClearButton** blocks, select the **ClearButton.Click** event. This block will help us clear out the list that stored the participants' phone numbers and the variable that stored the **WinningNumber**. Recall when we started coding the app, we initialized our global variables. We set **list** to be empty and the variable to be 0. So now, in the **when ClearButton.Click** event, add blocks to do the same thing. You've already programmed this once before in this app, so we imagine that you will be a pro at configuring these blocks again. But, just in case you need a review, select the **set global ListOfNumbers** block and connect it to the **create empty list** block, and select the **set global WinningNumber** block and set it to 0. Your final set of blocks will resemble the following screenshot:

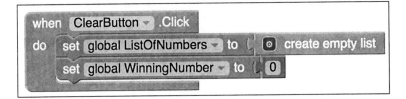

Summary

In this chapter, we created a useful and fun app that you can use to conduct a digital raffle. We explored global and local variables along with many facets of the Texting Component to send and receive text messages. We also learned about some advanced blocks related to lists—selecting random list items, searching for an item on a list, and removing an item. Finally, we explored an important fundamental concept of programming—loops. We saw how loops enabled us to repeat behaviors (a stack of blocks) multiple times.

In the next chapter, we will provide some tips on expanding your mobile app development skills with designing hints and sharing options.

8
Expanding Your Mobile App Development Skills

Throughout the tutorials in this book you have been increasing your app development skills. No doubt you are eager to build on this knowledge to embark on creating apps from scratch. Thus, we wanted to offer you a variety of tips for expanding your skill set. In this chapter you will learn about:

- Designing principles
- Designing tools
- Research app markets
- App Inventor extras
- Sharing your apps

Design principles

In addition to learning to code with blocks, there are many things to keep in mind when developing mobile apps. One important aspect is design. What do we mean by design? The word design seems to imply look and feel, but it also includes function. An app that is designed well is not only visually appealing, it is also easy to navigate and intuitive. When first building mobile apps, the tendency is to want your app to do it all and have lots of bells and whistles. But really, you want your app to be clear and straightforward in its function and purpose. Let's say you're building a book review app that shows user inputted reviews of books. You will not want it to also include music reviews. Just because your app is set up to easily add more categories doesn't mean you should add more content or features. When starting out, it is better to have a clear, precise purpose and scope for your app. And, because of the relatively small real estate of the mobile device screen, it is vitally important to have a clean, simple, and easy-to-navigate interface.

User-centered design

Think about the times you yourself have used a mobile app. Are you spending hours on just one app? Not likely. Most people use apps intermittently with a lot of interruptions. Rumor has it that people use mobile apps when they are busy, lost, or bored. The first two of these include the need for quick information, but the third does not necessarily imply extended usage. Someone bored could easily just need a quick fix to distract or entertain himself or herself for a few minutes. The best way to learn about design principles is to view Android apps through a developer's lens. Study how, when, and for how long people use mobile apps. Monitor your own app's behavior and ask others when they most often use apps. Is it when you're waiting in line? While traveling via public transport? Going to meet someone? How much time do you spend on one app before you move on to something else? Next, look analytically at apps—the ones you regularly use along with new ones. Examine everything—the fonts, the colors, and the placement of buttons or the navigation tools to see how they function and are displayed. Keep notes to track your discoveries, jotting down elements you expect to see and those that you find unexpected.

Keep in mind that mobile phone users will be navigating your app with their thumbs, so it is essential to make buttons big enough for easy navigation. If you make interactive elements too small and difficult to trigger, users could get frustrated and avoid using your app. Bottom navigation bars also make it easy for thumbs to control an app, which is why you will find this standard on many apps. Also, keep in mind that not all users have perfect vision. Create apps with high contrast colors and text that is easily viewed by people of all ages. It's a great idea to get a wide variety of people to view your app to give you feedback on things, such as colors, contrast, readability, and navigation ease.

Visual hierarchy

The way you display elements in terms of weight or importance is called **visual hierarchy**. You can create visual importance through the use of font size, colors, position, contrast, shape, or consistency. There are some Android elements that are familiar to users, such as an action bar that houses buttons to easily move about the app. Users will expect to find consistency on each screen along with ease in navigation. For example, it should be simple to stop, play, or quit at any point during a game app. In the Event App, we showed one way to make it apparent for the user to know which screen he or she is on by changing the text color of a button. You can also use other visual cues, such as highlighting a particular navigation button or creating a contrasting background color. Some of these recommendations may seem obvious, but you will be surprised to see how many people forget the obvious once they start creating apps from scratch.

Responsive design

Responsive design can refer to many things. Is your app responsive to users? Does it do what users think it will do? Does the app respond to user interaction as intended? Note that responsiveness and speed are not the same thing. It's OK if your app takes time to load something as long as the app is responding to user input and the user is aware that the app is responding. Responsive design also means that an app adjusts to a user's screen size. When creating apps, you don't know whether a user will have a mobile phone or tablet. What looks good on one screen size won't necessarily display properly on another, unless you ensure that it does. Responsive designing is creating layout and content for optimal viewing on any screen size. App Inventor makes it easy to do this. In the Properties panel of **Screen1**, there is a property called **Sizing**, as shown in the following screenshot. The default option is **Fixed**; but if you click on the word, a second option will be displayed: **Responsive**.

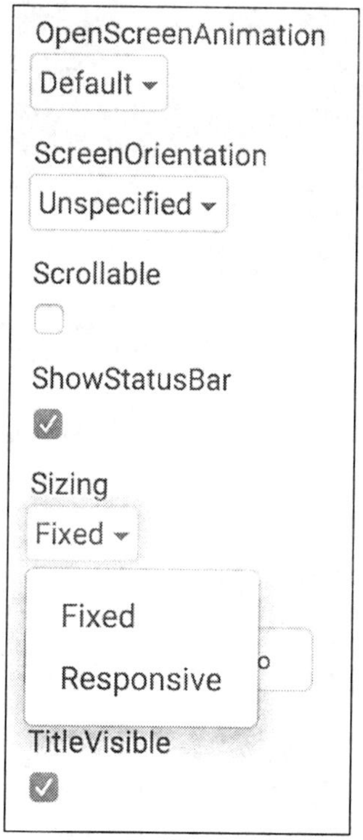

Upon choosing **Responsive**, a previously grayed out option in the **Viewer** will become visible. Immediately, above the **Viewer** window, you will now be able to click on the checkbox next to **Check to see Preview on Tablet size**. Once you do, the text will change to "un-check" and the Viewer will display a tablet preview of your app, as shown in the following screenshot with **EventApp**:

This is particularly helpful to view if you don't have a tablet and want to test how your app will look on one.

Research app markets

If you have the desire to make mobile apps from your own ideas, it is vital to understand the app market. How do you do this? You can do so by conducting research on mobile apps. Start looking at Google Play or other Android app markets and see what apps are new and popular. And most importantly, use those apps, jot down your reactions, what you liked and didn't like, and read reviews. Discover why certain apps in a category are more popular than others, what app features appeal to you, and also which types of apps are trending. Studying apps from the perspective of a developer will help you see themes in content, design, and user experience. Read descriptions of the apps to see how, for example, one chess game summary brands itself differently than other chess games. As we have recommended throughout this book, record your observations, reactions, and top picks, because like with any market, changes occur over time. It will be helpful for you to read what you noticed in the market 6 months ago and compare it to what your research revealed last week.

If you don't have a budget to buy apps, don't worry; you can still do valuable research on free apps or the ones that lead to in-app purchases. Notice what features are free and which ones are considered more valuable that they require a fee. When you get to the point of an in-app purchase, do you want to make one? Why or why not? Do the free apps have advertisements? If so, which apps? Which ads? If you do upgrade an app, what are the differences between the *freemium* and the paid versions of the same app?

This type of research will prove valuable when you complete this book and need help deciding what type of app to create on your own. The easiest way to find success creating apps is by giving users what they want. You can discover what users want by studying what apps are selling and popular. Many budding app developers fail to research app markets and instead just concentrate on coming up with an idea that they like and turning that concept into a prototype, hoping people will find the app, download it, use it, and like it. By paying attention to what users are already downloading and what they are willing to pay for, you can create an app with an understanding of what already appeals to users. Then, you can decide whether to follow this trend or disrupt it. Research can help ensure that your app is more successful once you upload it into app marketplaces. And the more people that use your apps, the more valuable feedback you will get. Ratings and comments can serve to help you improve subsequent versions or guide you in future app development.

Design tools

You can sketch out your app screens on index cards, notebook paper, poster size paper, or a whiteboard, or you can use some digital tools. There are a lot of free resources available to help you create paper or digital prototypes. Do a Google search for *paper prototyping for mobile apps*, or if you prefer the digital route, search for *wire framing for mobile apps* (note that we add the words *mobile apps* to our search because there are also a lot of resources for designing web pages). We even found a hybrid option (`https://popapp.in/`) that enables you to take pictures of your hand-drawn sketches and incorporate them into the app.

App Inventor extras

We'd like to introduce you to some App Inventor features that you may not know about.

Shortcuts

In this book, we showed you how to find and select blocks in the **Blocks** Editor. But, if you already know the block you want, there is a quick way to get it. All you have to do is click anywhere on the white space of the **Viewer** window and start typing. For example, if you want the **When GuestsButton.Click** event block, begin typing the word when and a drop-down list will appear, allowing you to choose the block you want among other blocks beginning with wh. Once you select the block, it will appear in the **Viewer**.

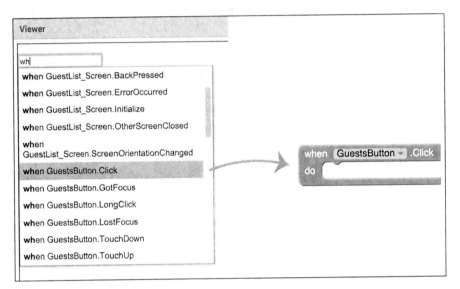

We didn't give you this shortcut initially because we wanted you to become familiar with where blocks were housed and how they were grouped (not because we wanted to make you work harder).

Help

There are a variety of ways to get help while you are using App Inventor. In the Designer, you may or may not have noticed little questions marks on the right-hand side of the Components Palette, as shown in the following screenshot:

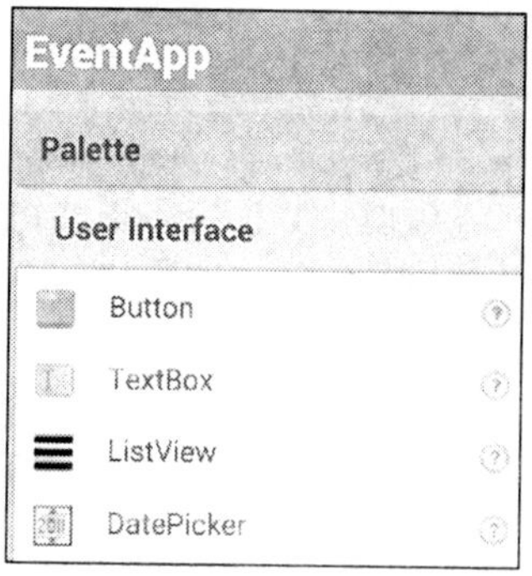

Clicking on a question mark launches a popup with information about a Component, as shown in the following screenshot:

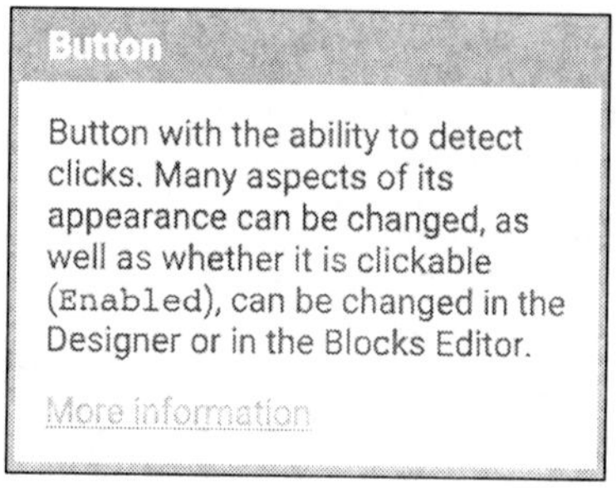

At the bottom of the window, you will see a **More information** link that will further direct you to documentation about that Component.

In the **Blocks** editor, you can easily find information about the blocks by hovering your cursor over a block. As shown in the following screenshots, hovering over different blocks launches a message revealing the block's purpose or type:

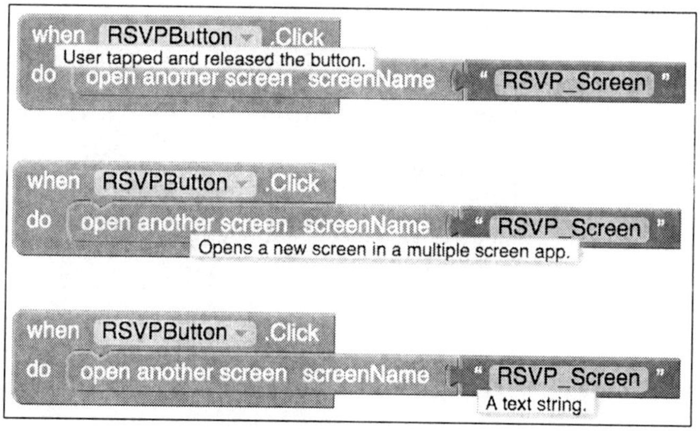

Another way to get help with App Inventor is to click on **Guide** in the top menu bar, as shown in the following screenshot:

My Projects	Gallery	Guide	Report an Issue	English ▾

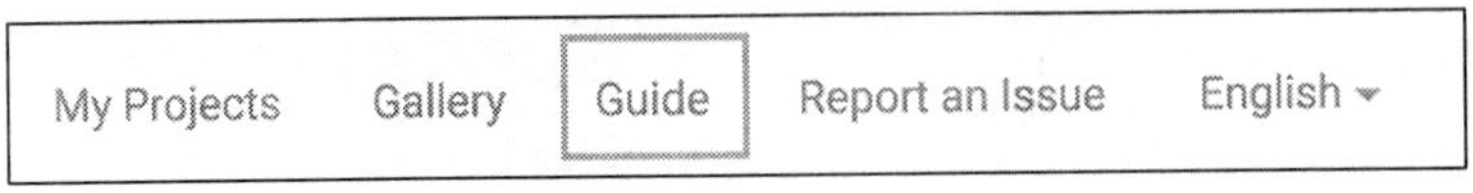

The **Guide** button will direct you to the App Inventor library of documentation. You can also access this website through `http://appinventor.mit.edu/explore/library`.

If you can't find an answer to a question or feel stuck, the **App Inventor Forum** is a way to interact with other users who have a wealth of experience with the platform. The link to the forum is found in the **Guide** documentation under **Support and Troubleshooting**.

Titles

While you can't change the name of **Screen1**, you can change the title of **Screen1** (or any screen for that matter) so that a different name will appear to the user. By default, **Title** is the name of **Screen1** (or if you are on a different screen, it will populate the screen name that you chose when creating the screen). Make sure you are on **Screen1** (if you have multiple screens) and select **Screen1** from the Components panel so that it is highlighted. Then, scroll to the very bottom of the Properties panel, as shown in the following screenshot. You will see the option of **Title**. Click on "Screen1" in the text box below; it will highlight the name and allow you to rename it. You will see the changes reflected at the top of the **Viewer** and also when you view the app on your device. You can retitle any screen with this method.

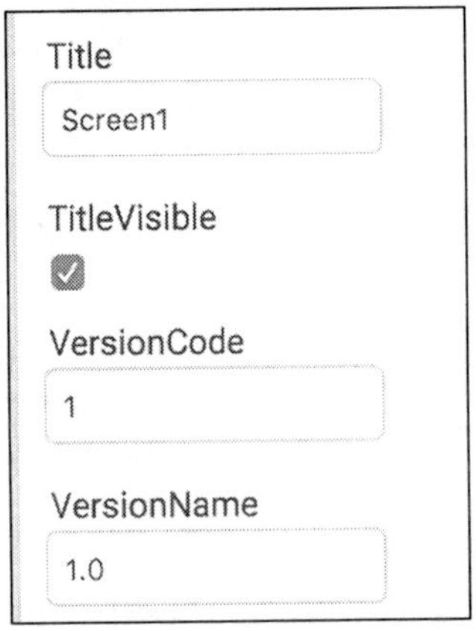

Title

Screen1

TitleVisible

☑

VersionCode

1

VersionName

1.0

Images

Currently, App Inventor has a 5 MB limit for the size of apps. This will not affect many of you at this point; but as you move farther along in your app development and create more complex apps, you may push up against this size limit. One thing that can help is reducing the size of any images. Be mindful to not use high-resolution images when creating your apps, as they take up a lot of space.

Virtual screens

In *Chapter 5, Building an Event App,* and *Chapter 6, Introduction to Databases,* we created the Event App that used four different screens. While being able to organize all your components in different screens is great for creating the visual hierarchy that any well-built app has, increasing the number of screens will ultimately increase the app's memory footprint, thereby reducing the performance. A small number (five or six) screens in an app is just fine. But as you keep on increasing the number of screens, you will get to a point where the app will start running a bit slow.

There is a workaround to have just one screen, but still have the visual hierarchy and the separation of components that you get by using multiple screens. The trick is to show or hide different components at different times to give the app user an illusion of multiple screens.

Let's say we are designing a simple form in our app. This form has two screens. In the first screen, the user types his/her name in a textbox and presses a button so that the name gets added to some sort of data storage (list, TinyDB, Fusion Table, and so on). When the user presses the button, the second screen opens up and shows a confirmation message. The second screen also has a button to go back to the first screen.

Instead of creating two separate screens, we can create this behavior using a virtual single screen. The following screenshot shows all the components and how they are placed:

The interesting thing that you might notice is that we have placed all the components within two different vertical arrangements. We have placed all the components that we want on **Screen1** in **VerticalArrangement1** and all the components that we want on **Screen2** in **VerticalArrangement2**. When the app starts, we will keep **VerticalArragnement1** visible and hide **VerticalArrangement2** (hiding, or making it invisible, automatically makes all the components inside a vertical arrangement invisible too). Then, whenever the user presses the button to enter a name, we will hide **VerticalArrangement1** and show **VerticalArrangement2**. Subsequently, when the user presses the button to go back, we will show **VerticalArrangement1** and hide **VerticalArrangement2**.

In other words, we will toggle between showing one of the vertical arrangements and hiding the other. This will give the user an illusion of multiple screens even though the app has a single screen.

Let's explore all the details of this. Here are the steps that you need to implement in the Designer:

1. Go to the **Properties** panel of **Screen1**, and change the **Title** property from **Screen1** to something else. As shown in the following screenshot, we have changed it to **Virtual screen demo**:

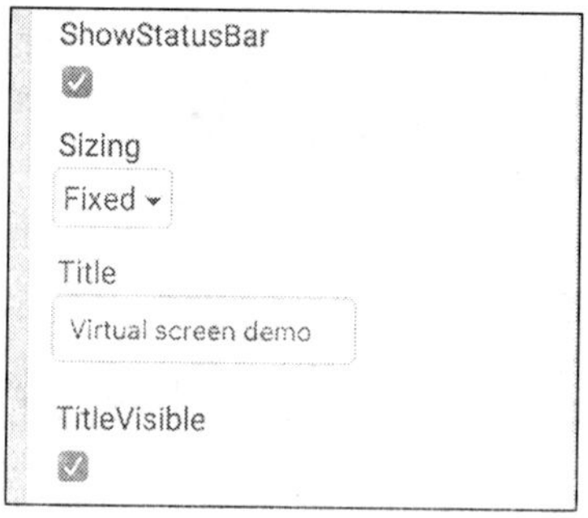

2. Next, add two vertical arrangements. Make the **Height** and the **Width** properties of both the vertical arrangements **Fill parent**. This will make both of them span the entire width of **Screen1** and make each one's height half of **Screen1**, as shown in the following screenshot:

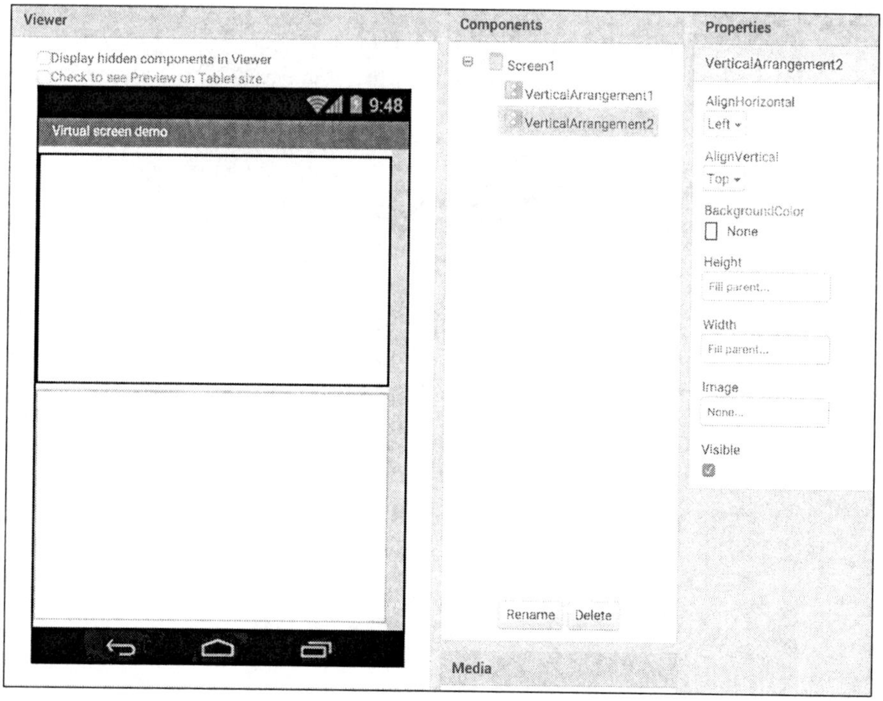

3. Now, in **VerticalArrangement 1**, add a Label, a Textbox, and a Button. Change the **Text** property of **Label1** to **Enter your name:**. Delete the **Hint** property of **TextBox1**. Finally, change the **Text** property of **Button1** to **Enter**. The following screenshot shows the result of completing this step:

4. In **VerticalArrangement 2**, add a label and a button. App Inventor will automatically name them **Label2** and **Button2**. Delete the **Text** property of **Label2** and keep it empty. Change the **Text** property of **Button2** to **Go Back**. Your **Viewer** will look as follows:

5. Finally, uncheck the **Visible** property of **VerticalArrangement2**. This will hide **VerticalArrangement2** and all the components in it. When you do this, your designer will look as follows:

Switch to the **Blocks** Editor to create the behavior — toggling between showing and hiding the two vertical arrangements to create the illusion of multiple screens. Follow these steps:

1. When the user clicks on **Button1** (the button that says **Enter**), you will need to perform the following steps:

   1. Hide VerticalArrangement1 by setting the **VerticalArrangement1. Visible** property to **false**.

   2. Show VerticalArrangement2 by setting the **VerticalArrangement2. Visible** property to **true**.

   3. Get the text from **TextBox1** by using the **TextBox1.Text** getter block, join this text with a blank Text block filled with **"You Entered: "**. Set **Label2** by setting **Label2.Text to** the result of the **join** block.

   4. Clear TextBox1 by setting the **TextBox1.Text** property to an empty string.

   The following screenshot shows the blocks that achieve steps *a* to *d*:

2. When a user clicks on **Button2** (the button that says **Go Back**), you will do the reverse of steps 1*a* and 1*b*, that is:

   1. Show VerticalArrangement1 by setting the **VerticalArrangement1. Visible** property to **true**.

   2. Hide VerticalArrangement2 by setting the **VerticalArrangement2. Visible** property to **false**.

   The following screenshot shows the blocks that achieve steps 2*a* and 2*b*:

When you test this app or when the app first launches, you will see **VerticalArrangement1** and all its components, as shown in the following screenshot:

When you enter a name in **TextBox1** and click on the button that says **Enter**, you will see the following screenshot:

Finally, when you click on the button that says **Go Back**, you will see what you saw first when the app launched. This is how you create an illusion of multiple screens while actually only having a single screen, thereby reducing the memory requirements of the app and making the app more efficient.

Backups

App Inventor automatically saves your app as you are creating it. Even though you will see a **Save project** option under the Projects menu, rest assured that your app is regularly saved by the platform. However, as you build apps, saving a copy of your progress is extremely important in case you want to revert to an earlier version or, for example, you wish to examine your code before you encounter a bug to determine what went wrong. One option in the drop-down list under the **Projects** menu is **Save project as...** (as shown in the following screenshot on the left-hand side). This option lets you create a second copy of your project with a new name. Then, the new copy will become your current working project.

On the other hand, using the **Checkpoint** option regularly throughout development provides a way to create backups in a systematic manner while continuing to work on the same version of the app. When you choose **Checkpoint** (as shown in the following screenshot on the right-hand side) under the **Projects** menu, App Inventor will seamlessly create backups behind the scenes. For instance, our Event App versions would be saved as **EventApp_Checkpoint1**, **EventApp_Checkpoint2**, and so on. This way, you can open any version of the Event App at varying stages throughout development. Once you finish your app and create your final version, you can delete the **Checkpoint** versions, as you will no longer need them.

Distributing your app

We are sure you've noticed, either in an app store or on your device, that all the apps have icons. This small image enables users to easily recognize one app from another. Before sharing your app, you will want to upload an icon. This could be some artwork that you used in your app or a logo if you have created one. You can easily upload this image in the **Properties** panel for **Screen1** under the option **Icon**. You will find it midway down the panel of options.

The App Inventor Gallery

Whether you've made an app with the help of a tutorial or from scratch, you have the privilege of sharing your app with others. There are many ways to do this. The easiest way is from within App Inventor itself with the **Gallery**.

Viewing the Gallery apps

You may have noticed a menu item called **Gallery**, as shown in the next screenshot:

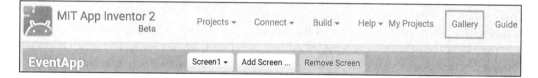

If you click on the Gallery button, you can peruse many remarkable apps that other people have shared. Not only can you view apps to get inspiration, but you can use the Gallery as a learning tool because you can view the source codes of any of the apps in it. Click on an app icon that looks interesting or the one that you would like to learn how to build and it will launch a window with a button **OPEN THE APP**.

Click on the button and a pop-up box will appear to save the app or rename it, as shown in the following screenshot:

This method saves the app to your Projects list, and you can open the file and examine the UI in the Designer and the code in the **Blocks** Editor to see how the app was made. You can remix the app by adding or changing blocks to create your own version of the app, or you can copy some of the existing blocks into the **Backpack** and load them into another project that you are working on (Blocks saved in the Backpack can be accessed by any of your projects and remain there until you quit App Inventor). This is a great way to learn new code, discover ways that other people built apps and learn the art of remixing projects.

Sharing your app in the Gallery

Since the Gallery is an open resource tool for learning and collaborating, keep in mind you have to be okay with the practice of sharing your own code with others. To share your app with others in the **Gallery**, click on the **My Projects** button in the top menu bar and select the app you would like to share by clicking on the checkbox next to the app name. When you do this, two buttons that were once grayed out become active (the **Delete Project** button and the **Publish to Gallery** button), as shown in the following screenshots:

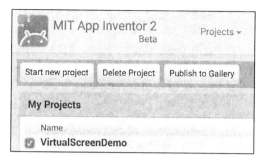

When you publish to the **Gallery**, you can opt to receive e-mails that notify you when your app has been downloaded and liked. You can also obtain a link to share, which will direct others to your app. Getting feedback on your app before publishing it on the Google Play Store is a great way to test the market.

Creating an AIA file

An .aia file is the file type you will need to create when sharing an app in the Gallery or with someone else. This file type allows you to load an app into your project's list and examine the UI and source code. It is also useful when you are collaborating on a project with someone else or if you want a specific person to take a look at your code. Within App Inventor, it is easy to make an .aia file to share with someone else.

Click on the **Projects** button in the menu bar and select the eighth option from the drop-down menu, **Export selected project (.aia) to my computer**, as shown in the following screenshot:

This action will place the file in your `Downloads` folder (or in another location that you designate). You can send the `.aia` file to a collaborator by attaching the file in an e-mail. The recipient will first download the file to his or her computer (into the `Downloads` folder) and then easily upload the file to his or her App Inventor project list by selecting the third option in the previous image, **Import project (.aia) from my computer**.

When publishing an app to the Google Play Store, it is highly recommended that you save an extra copy of your own source code and store it in a safe place. You will most likely create new versions and updates of your app, so it is recommended to keep copies of your app files in the unlikely event that anything were to happen to the copy on App Inventor. Follow the previous steps to **Export selected project (.aia) to my computer** and then copy the `.aia` file to a flash drive or hard drive.

Downloading and sharing

So far with our app development, we have been working inside of App Inventor—both when building and live testing our app and now while sharing it in the Gallery. But, when you create your own app from scratch, it makes sense to download your app and test it on as many devices as possible before you widely distribute it. To download your app to your device or to make it available for others to download, you have a few options.

Regardless of which option you decide to use, to ensure that your device allows file downloads other than those from the Google Play Store, you may have to adjust your mobile device settings. You may recall that we explained the step of side-loading in *Chapter 2, Setting Up MIT App Inventor 2*, when we provided instructions for directly downloading the AI2 Companion App. We suggest that you follow these steps to ensure that your device can install apps from **unknown sources**. For devices with Honeycomb or earlier, go to **Settings** | **Applications** and enable **Unknown Sources** by checking the box. For Ice Cream Sandwich and later versions, go to **Settings** | **Security** or **Settings** | **Security & Screen Lock** to check the box for **Unknown Sources**.

Creating an APK

> When distributing your app in an app market like the Google Play Store, you will not be sharing your source code, so you need a file type other than an `.aia` file. In this case, you will build out your app into an `.apk` file. This is easily done in App Inventor.

There are two options for creating an `.apk` file: using a QR code or side-loading.

QR code

Click on the **Build** button in the top menu bar and choose the first option from the drop-down menu: **App (provide QR code for .apk)**, as shown in the following screenshot:

This will launch the build process, and after a few moments, a QR code will appear on your computer screen. *Do not scan this with the AI2 Companion app, as it will not work.* You will need to scan the code with a QR code reader on your mobile device. Many free QR code reader apps are available on the Google Play Store; you can find one by doing a search. The QR code is only available for a certain time period, so be mindful of the time limit noted, as in the following screenshot:

Once you have scanned the QR code with your mobile device, click on **Open** to begin the download process. You will next see an installation screen asking **Do you want to install this application? If so, it will get access to:**. And you will see a list of items on the device that the app needs to access. This list is determined by the components in the app. Since you created this app, you can easily agree to the permissions. Click on **Install**. Once the installation is complete, your app will be stored on your device; you can locate it in the same location as the other apps on your device.

Direct download (or side-loading)

To download an `.apk` file directly to your computer, click on the **Build** menu option and choose the second option, **App (save .apk to my computer)**.

The file will take a moment to build and will either save to your `Downloads` folder or to a location that you designate. You can easily locate your file in a search because the name will end with the extension `.apk`. To get your app to your mobile device, you have a few options. You can do the following:

- Connect your Android mobile device to your computer via USB and drag the file to the phone or tablet icon to copy it.

- Send the file to yourself by attaching it to an e-mail and then opening the e-mail on your mobile device and downloading the file to your device.

- Upload the file to a shared web storage location, such as Google Drive, (since it is connected to your Google account) and then access the file through your device. To do this, you would need to either have the Google Drive app on your device or sign into your account on your phone by using the web address: `http://drive.google.com`. Once you open Google Drive on your device, locate your .apk file and open it.

Regardless of which method you use, once you click on the file to open it, you will be shown the (aforementioned) installation screen asking **Do you want to install this application? If so, it will get access to:**. Click on **Install**. Once the installation is complete, your app will be stored on your device; you can locate it in the same location as the other apps on your device.

The Google Play Store

There are a few things in App Inventor that you may have not noticed previously that you need to be mindful of at the stage when you are considering publishing to the Google Play Store. Apps published in Google Play need both **VersionCode** and **VersionName**. Both of these can be found in the Designer window of App Inventor at the bottom of the **Properties** panel for **Screen1**, as shown in the following screenshot:

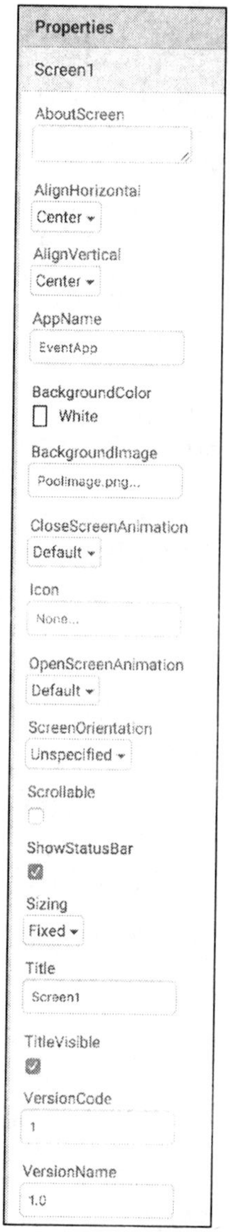

Properties
Screen1

AboutScreen

AlignHorizontal
Center ▾

AlignVertical
Center ▾

AppName
EventApp

BackgroundColor
☐ White

BackgroundImage
Poolimage.png...

CloseScreenAnimation
Default ▾

Icon
None...

OpenScreenAnimation
Default ▾

ScreenOrientation
Unspecified ▾

Scrollable
☐

ShowStatusBar
☑

Sizing
Fixed ▾

Title
Screen1

TitleVisible
☑

VersionCode
1

VersionName
1.0

These properties are needed by both Google Play and Android to keep track of updates to ensure that the user has the most recent version of an app. Every time you submit a new version of an app, **VersionCode** must be a greater whole number than the previous version. **VersionName** does not have to be numerical, but it should be consistent among versions because the user will see this information. To begin the Google Play Store publishing process, go into your App Inventor projects, select the app you would like to distribute on Google Play, build the .apk file, and download it to your computer.

Next, make sure you're logged into your Google account and visit `http://play.google.com/apps/publish`. This link will take you to the Google Play Developer Console, and the first thing you will need to do is sign up for a Developer Account, which costs a fee. Since Google makes changes to the process occasionally, we are going to recommend that you visit the App Inventor website documentation `http://appinventor.mit.edu/explore/ai2/google-play.html` to get the most up-to-date steps on how to publish to Google Play.

One thing to note, Google Play gives you three options for publishing: Alpha or Beta testing or Production. Once you have a finished app, we are certain you will be anxious to share your app with the world; but even if you have done a fair share of testing on your own, we recommend taking yet another opportunity to continue testing. **Alpha** testing is a small group that you can designate, **Beta** testing is testing with a bigger but limited audience, and of course, **Production** shares the app with the public. Each time you make a new version, we recommend testing it out on your Alpha and Beta testers before you send it out to production.

Summary

This book has provided you with ideas, tools, tutorials, and guidance to become a mobile app developer with MIT App Inventor. You've learned how to do the following:

- Perform a technical setup for App Inventor
- Brainstorm app ideas using the Design Thinking process
- Conduct app research during both the idea generating stage and in the prototype phase
- Navigate the App Inventor platform
- Create a user interface keeping design principles in mind
- Build a user-touch game, an event app, and a raffle app, and expand upon them with more complex features
- Code blocks using sequences, if/then statements, multiple screens, virtual screens, images, databases, and loops
- Research the app marketplace
- Share your apps with others

As you have experienced, a lot of time, effort, iteration, dedication, and creativity goes into making mobile applications. We are certain that the content shared in this book has sparked more than just a casual interest in mobile app development. You have learned skills in coding and design, both of which will help you embark on your new role as an app developer. No doubt you are hooked on making apps and intend to expand your skills even further. The possibilities for creating social impactful apps are indeed endless and we hope that the coding, design, research, and entrepreneurial skills you learned in this book launch you into becoming a lifelong technology creator!

Index

A

ActivityStarter, event app
  adding 130-132
AI2 companion app
  downloading 27, 28
AIA file
  creating 217, 218
aiStarter
  starting 41
alpha testing 222
Android developer instructions
  URL 40
APK, creating options
  direct download (or side-loading) 220
  QR code 219
App Inventor, features
  about 203
  backups 214
  help 204-206
  images 207
  shortcuts 204
  titles 206
  URL 222
  virtual screens 207-214
apps, distributing
  about 215
  AIA file, creating 217, 218
  APK, creating 218
  app, sharing in Gallery 217
  downloading and sharing 218
  Gallery 215
  Gallery apps, viewing 215, 216
  Google Play Store 220-222

B

background image, event app
  setting 120-123
Backpack tool 135
beta testing 222
Blocks editor
  about 71, 72
  Blocks drawer 72
blocks, event app
  programming 134
  screen 1 134
  screens and launching maps,
      navigating between 134
  sharing between screens,
      Backpack used 135-137
  text, adding to screens 138
blocks, types
  about 73
  event blocks 73
  getters 73
  setters 73
blocks, used for program Fling
  ball, bouncing 83-89
  ball, flinging 82
  ball, moving 78-81
  game, encoding 83-89
  Play button 73-78
  Reset button 90, 92
Brain Reaction Accelerator 14
buttons, event app
  adding 126-130
BYJ3S 12

C

connectivity setup, MIT App Inventor 2
  about 27
  AI2 companion app, downloading 27, 28
  aiStarter, starting 41
  App Inventor setup software, installing 31
  App Inventor setup software, installing
      for GNU/Linux 39
  App Inventor setup software, installing
      for Mac OS X 32-34
  App Inventor setup software, installing
      for Windows 34-39
  computer and Android device, connecting
      with WiFi 29, 30
  computer and device, connecting 44
  Debian package , installing instructions 40
  device, setting up for USB cable 43
  emulator, connecting 31
  emulator, project connecting to 41, 42
  GNU/Linux systems , installing
      instructions 40
  project, opening 41, 42
  testing 45
  USB cable, used for connection 31
Construction Calculator 15
**CSAIL (Computer Science and Artificial
      Intelligence Lab) 2**

D

data
  pushing, to Fusion Table 164, 165
  receiving 169, 170
  requesting 169, 170
database
  creating 142
  Google Fusion Table, creating 142-145
designer
  about 49
  components 50
  media 51
  palette 50
  properties 51
  viewer 50
design principles, mobile app
  about 199
  design tools 203

  research 202, 203
  responsive design 201, 202
  user centered design 200
  visual hierarchy 200
Design Thinking process
  about 4, 5
  define 6
  ideate 6
  prototype 7
  test 7

E

event app
  ActivityStarter, adding 130-132
  background Image, setting 120-123
  blocks, programming 134
  buttons, adding 126-130
  image component, adding 124, 125
  screens, adding 133
  sharing 171, 172
  user interface 120
Ez School Bus Locator 17

F

Fling app
  about 93
  difficulty, increasing 100
  dynamic, changing 101-103
  levels, creating 103-107
  Play button, updating 115
  Reset button, updating 111-114
  score label updating, to display
      labels 108-110
  scoring feature, adding 95
Fusion Table
  app, connecting to 161, 162
  blocks, creating 169
  creating 142-149
  data, pushing 164-166
  data, receiving 169, 170
  data, requesting 169
  empty rows 166, 167
  guest list, viewing 168
  sharing, with service account
      email 159, 160

G

Gallery apps
  viewing 215, 216
game
  dynamic, changing 101-103
game app
  creating 51, 52
  Integrated Development Environment
      (IDE) 60-70
  UI in designer, creating 52-59
Google Authentication
  setting up 153-159
Google Fusion Table. *See* Fusion Table
Google Play Store 220-222
Graphical User Interface (GUI) 26
guest list
  viewing 168

I

image component, event app
  adding 124, 125
Integrated Development Environment
    (IDE) 52, 60-70

L

levels
  creating 103-108
library
  URL 206
license types
  URL 122
Loops 13

M

MIT App Inventor
  Brain Reaction Accelerator 14
  BYJ3S 12
  ConstHelp 15
  examples 11
  Ez School Bus Locator 17
  Loops 13
  possibilities, discovering 10
  potential 9, 10
  purpose 9, 10

  Quartet 14
  Rover 800 Remote 18
  Stopwatch and Timer 11
  Umati 16
  Yahtzee 12
  Youth Radio 17
MIT App Inventor 2
  about 1, 2
  app designing, best practices 8, 9
  app ideas, brainstorming 4
  computational thinking 8
  connectivity setup 27
  Design Thinking process 4
  Google account, signing up 23
  initial setup 22
  logging into 23-27
  mobile app developer role 3
  system, requisites 22
  URL 2, 7, 23
mobile app
  design principles 199

P

Play button
  updating 115
project view
  about 48
  new project, creating 48

Q

QR code 219
Quartet 14

R

Raffle app
  digital Raffle app, behavior
      programming 179
  everyone else, notifying 190-192
  GUI, building 174
  list and variable, clearing out 196
  loops, using 193-196
  new project, creating 174
  phone numbers of all participants,
      adding to list 185, 186
  project, creating 174

text messages, receiving from
      participants 182-184
User Interface (UI), creating 175-178
winner, notifying 189
winner, selecting 187, 188
Reset button
  updating 111-114
Rover 800 Remote 18
RSVP screen
  designing 149
  GUI, creating in designer window 149-152

S

score label
  updating, to display level 108-110
scoring feature
  adding 95
  score label, updating 98
  scoring blocks, coding 95-98
service account email
  Fusion Table, sharing 159, 160
sizing property 201
Stopwatch and Timer 11

U

Umati 16

V

visual hierarchy 200

Y

Yahtzee 12
Youth Radio 17

CPSIA information can be obtained
at www.ICGtesting.com
Printed in the USA
FFOW01n1253301116
29930FF